The Agentic AI Revolution

Leveraging Microsoft AI and Autonomous Agents to Transform Work and Business

Will Hawkins
Nancie Calder

Apress®

The Agentic AI Revolution: Leveraging Microsoft AI and Autonomous Agents to Transform Work and Business

Will Hawkins
Toronto, Canada

Nancie Calder
Toronto, Canada

ISBN-13 (pbk): 979-8-8688-2021-2
https://doi.org/10.1007/979-8-8688-2022-9

ISBN-13 (electronic): 979-8-8688-2022-9

Copyright © 2025 by Will Hawkins, Nancie Calder

This work is subject to copyright. All rights are reserved by the Publisher, whether the whole or part of the material is concerned, specifically the rights of translation, reprinting, reuse of illustrations, recitation, broadcasting, reproduction on microfilms or in any other physical way, and transmission or information storage and retrieval, electronic adaptation, computer software, or by similar or dissimilar methodology now known or hereafter developed.

Trademarked names, logos, and images may appear in this book. Rather than use a trademark symbol with every occurrence of a trademarked name, logo, or image we use the names, logos, and images only in an editorial fashion and to the benefit of the trademark owner, with no intention of infringement of the trademark.

The use in this publication of trade names, trademarks, service marks, and similar terms, even if they are not identified as such, is not to be taken as an expression of opinion as to whether or not they are subject to proprietary rights.

While the advice and information in this book are believed to be true and accurate at the date of publication, neither the authors nor the editors nor the publisher can accept any legal responsibility for any errors or omissions that may be made. The publisher makes no warranty, express or implied, with respect to the material contained herein.

Managing Director, Apress Media LLC: Welmoed Spahr
Acquisitions Editor: Smriti Srivastava
Coordinating Editor: Jessica Vakili

Distributed to the book trade worldwide by Springer Science+Business Media New York, 1 New York Plaza, New York, NY 10004. Phone 1-800-SPRINGER, fax (201) 348-4505, e-mail orders-ny@springer-sbm.com, or visit www.springeronline.com. Apress Media, LLC is a Delaware LLC and the sole member (owner) is Springer Science + Business Media Finance Inc (SSBM Finance Inc). SSBM Finance Inc is a **Delaware** corporation.

For information on translations, please e-mail booktranslations@springernature.com; for reprint, paperback, or audio rights, please e-mail bookpermissions@springernature.com.

Apress titles may be purchased in bulk for academic, corporate, or promotional use. eBook versions and licenses are also available for most titles. For more information, reference our Print and eBook Bulk Sales web page at http://www.apress.com/bulk-sales.

Any source code or other supplementary material referenced by the author in this book is available to readers on GitHub (https://github.com/Apress). For more detailed information, please visit https://www.apress.com/gp/services/source-code.

If disposing of this product, please recycle the paper

To our families,
We can't thank you enough for all you do and all you are. It is such a privilege to share all aspects of our lives with you and we're truly grateful for your unwavering commitment and support.

To our friends and colleagues,
We want you to know how much we appreciate the immense influence you've had on what we're writing about. Thank you for supporting, caring, and appreciating what we're doing, and why we're doing it, from start to finish. This book and the stories within would not be possible without your presence in both of our lives and careers.

To the reader,

We're grateful you picked up this story, not because we appreciate you consuming our literary work, but because you just made one of the most important decisions of your life. To immerse yourself in a world that is partially here and partially on its way. We are honored to get to share these insights with you and hope that it empowers you to take your future to places you never thought possible.

Table of Contents

About the Authors ix

About the Technical Reviewer xi

Acknowledgments xiii

Prologue xv

Chapter 1: The AI Landscape and Its Evolving Impact 1

    1.1 From Novelty to Necessity: A Brief History of AI Evolution 1

    1.2 Automation, Augmentation, and the Rise of Collaboration 4

    1.3 Democratization of AI: From Developers to Power Users 7

    1.4 New Business Models and Economic Shifts 8

    1.5 The Human–AI Relationship: Partner, Tool, or Threat? 11

    1.6 Role-Based Vignettes: Agents in Action Across the Enterprise 12

    1.7 Leadership Checklist: Embracing Agentic AI in Your Organization 14

Chapter 2: Challenges and Gaps in Current AI Adoption 17

    2.1 The Limits of Traditional Automation 18

    2.2 Why Context Matters: The Weakness of Static Models 20

    2.3 The Black Box Problem: Why Trust Breaks Down 22

    2.4 Siloed Intelligence: Fragmentation Across Tools 24

    2.5 Resource Intensive and Fragile to Change 25

    2.6 Missing the Human Element 27

    2.7 Why Agentic AI Is the Next Step Forward and Its Emerging Risks 28

TABLE OF CONTENTS

Chapter 3: Understanding Agency—What Makes Agentic AI a Teammate, Not a Tool 33

   3.1 From Pins To Prompts: How Adam Smith's 250-Year-Old Theory Is Driving the Agentic AI Revolution 35

   3.2 What Makes Something Agentic? 37

      The Three Pillars of Agency 38

   3.3 Degrees of Freedom: A Taxonomy 41

      Scenario A—*The HR Help Hub* 49

      Scenario B—Overnight Ledger Reconciler 50

      Scenario C—Sales-Forecast Orchestrator 50

   3.4 Digital Division-of-Labor Playbook 51

      Order-to-Cash in Four Digital Specialists 55

   3.5 Bringing the Pieces Together 57

Chapter 4: Why Agentic Capabilities Outperform Traditional AI 59

   4.1 Benchmark 1: Task Robustness 61

   4.2 Benchmark 2: Self-Directed Problem Solving 63

   4.3 Benchmark 3: Automating Iteration 64

   4.4 Agent Swarms: Coordinated Autonomy at Scale 66

   4.5 Quantifying Impact: Productivity, Quality, Speed 68

Chapter 5: Microsoft's AI Stack and Agentic Evolution 75

   5.1 Meet the Ecosystem: Copilot, Azure AI, Power Platform, Fabric 76

      The Infrastructure Foundation (Figure 5-1—Bottom Circle) 77

      Data and Orchestration (Figure 5-1—Data Orchestration Circle) 78

      AI Service Suite (Figure 5-1—AI Service Suite Circle) 78

      Business Applications Layer (Figure 5-1—Business Applications Circle) 81

   5.2 Deciding Which Layer to Use 83

      Focus on Mapping Where Your Data Lives to Each Tool's Connector Framework 84

      Not Every Agent Needs to Interact with a User Through Conversation 84

      Start at the Top and Drill Deeper 85

   5.3 Agentic Framework: Tool Combination Deep Dives 87

      Implementing Copilot Studio 87

    Azure AI Agent Service Patterns That Will Have You Wiring Agents Together Like A Pro 88

    Hardening the Business Applications Layer for AI Success.. 90

  5.4 Success Stories and Real World Applications 91

Chapter 6: Governing Agentic AI—Principles, Practices, and Playbooks............... 99

  6.1 Why Governance Matters for Agentic AI 100

  6.2 Core Principles for Responsible Agentic AI 102

  6.3 Designing a Governance Framework 105

  6.4 Building Governance Playbooks... 106

  6.5 Challenges and Pitfalls... 109

  6.6 From Compliance to Competitive Edge 110

  6.7 The Future of AI Governance 112

Chapter 7: Embracing the Agentic Workforce 117

  7.1 The Human Side of the Agentic Revolution 118

  7.2 Building AI Fluency and Capabilities That Scale 120

  7.3 Evolving the Employee Experience 122

  7.4 Change Management for Agentic Transformation.. 124

  7.5 Leadership for the Age of Agents... 125

  7.6 Aligning Organizational Design to Support AI.. 127

  7.7 Scaling Sustainably... 129

Chapter 8: Beyond the Horizon 133

  8.1 The Autonomy Maturity Path 136

  8.2 Scaling Agentic AI—From Pilots to Enterprise Flight... 139

  8.3 Practicing Ethical AI: Harmonizing Innovation and Responsibility 141

  8.4 Maximizing the Human in the Loop.. 142

  8.5 Positioning for the Future: Orienting to an AI-First Business Model 144

  8.6 Beyond the Agent Era—Glimpsing the Next Horizon 146

  8.7 Conclusion: Embracing the Horizon 147

Index.. 151

About the Authors

Will Hawkins is an Azure AI and Microsoft Fabric Engineer, as well as a Data Scientist by trade, with a deep-rooted background in AI and machine learning—long before "Copilot" became synonymous with AI applications. Over the past four years, Will has been on a journey of self-realization and self-actualization through the lens of the world's data. Beginning his career as an Econometrician with Statistics Canada, he later became the Lead Digital Twins Expert for Healthcare at Avanade, followed by a role as Lead AI Expert at ITRAK 365. These experiences laid the foundation for founding his own company, RitewAI.

For the past two years, Will has been building RitewAI into a leading firm specializing in Microsoft's AI stack. Leveraging deep expertise across Microsoft Fabric, Azure AI, and the Power Platform, RitewAI empowers Microsoft ISVs, partners, and customers to drive AI innovation through consulting, engineering, and strategic advisory services. Will was also recently recognized as a Copilot Studio MVP and just finished publishing his first book, *AI Essentials Guide: Principles for Navigating the Next Tech Renaissance*.

Nancie Calder is an executive at Avanade Inc., where she leads the global Dynamics 365 CRM Practice. Since joining Avanade in 2014, Nancie has held several leadership roles,

working closely with both business and IT executive teams to drive positive outcomes through the adoption of innovative technologies like AI.

Prior to her time at Avanade, Nancie spent over 20 years as an independent information technology consultant. During that time, she supported her own clients and worked with various consulting firms. Her roles have ranged from fractional CIO to executive at a software company later acquired by Microsoft. In recent years, Nancie has focused on mentoring IT professionals through her work as a Dynamics 365 Contact Center MVP, drawing from her broad and deep experience across the tech landscape. She is passionate about excellence, embraces new challenges and technology, and is dedicated to helping others succeed in their careers.

About the Technical Reviewer

Kasam Shaikh is a prominent figure in India's artificial intelligence landscape, holding the distinction of being one of the country's first four Microsoft Most Valuable Professionals (MVPs) in AI. Currently serving as a Chief Architect, Kasam boasts an impressive track record as an author, having authored five best-selling books dedicated to Azure and AI technologies. Beyond his writing endeavors, Kasam is recognized as a Microsoft Certified Trainer (MCT), Career AI Expert Guru, and influential tech YouTuber (@ mekasamshaikh). He also leads the largest online Azure AI community, known as Dear Azure | Azure INDIA, and is a globally renowned AI speaker. His commitment to knowledge sharing extends to contributions to Microsoft Learn, where he plays a pivotal role.

Within the realm of AI, Kasam is a respected Subject Matter Expert (SME) in Generative AI for the Cloud, complementing his role as a Chief Architect. He actively promotes the adoption of No Code and Azure OpenAI solutions and possesses a strong foundation in Hybrid and Cross-Cloud practices. Kasam Shaikh's versatility and expertise make him an invaluable asset in the rapidly evolving landscape of technology, contributing significantly to the advancement of Azure and AI.

In summary, Kasam Shaikh is a multifaceted professional who excels in both technical expertise and knowledge dissemination. His contributions span writing, training, community leadership, public speaking, and architecture, establishing him as a true luminary in the world of Azure and AI. Kasam was recently awarded as top voice in AI by LinkedIn, making him the sole exclusive Indian professional acknowledged by both Microsoft and LinkedIn for his contributions to the world of Artificial Intelligence!

Acknowledgments

We are so grateful for the universe blessing us with the opportunity to share this gift of knowledge at this place in time and space.

It is also our great privilege to have worked with the incredible Apress team and its wonderful leaders and constituents.

Finally, we extend our gratitude to members of various communities, especially the Dynamics User Group community, the Dynamics Communities community, as well as the entire Microsoft partner ecosystem, for generously sharing their knowledge.

To everyone who, directly or indirectly, contributed through countless conversations about AI—where it has been, where it is today, and where it is heading—we extend our deepest thanks.

Prologue

Welcome!

First of all, thank you for taking the time to sit down and give this book a go. It has become a rare gift to seek out and put time and attention into reading something that has the ability to change your life.

We're not saying that because this is some kind of holy scripture on the philosophy of AI Agents. But because we truly believe that the stories we share in this narrative have the potential to change the way you think and operate in a positive manner.

Why do we believe in this so strongly?

Will: Five years ago I hit the lowest point in my life. Stumbling onto the field of artificial intelligence—systems that could learn, reason, and even converse—showed me a reality bigger than the one I was trapped in. Modeling human behavior with data and machines became more than a career goal; it became a way to rebuild my understanding of how the mind worked and use this to change how the world thinks and operates.

Nancie: I have chased the promise of behavioral modeling for decades. Long before today's tools existed, I standardized data wherever I could, waiting for the moment we'd have enough horsepower to unlock its value. In CRM, that dream took shape as the 360-degree customer view: every interaction, preference, and transaction stitched into a single, living profile that lets businesses serve people as individuals—not segments.

That is what this book aims to be. Not just content on AI Agents in the Microsoft Ecosystem, but an exploration into what's truly possible today. How we can re-shape our understanding of the human role in day-to-day life, organizations, enterprises, and global economies. How we get to decide what we want to maintain ownership of and what we're comfortable with delegating to our AI companions. And most importantly, how we can scale the human in the loop by giving them a healthy supply of well-architected AI agents to supercharge their capabilities.

In order to accomplish this, we're going to take you through a journey that the two of us have been on for quite some time. We're going to start by walking you through not only what we've witnessed in the last couple of years of the GenAI era, but in the three decades prior that has led to this tectonic shift in possibility.

PROLOGUE

We'll then take you through the challenges and gaps with AI adoption today. What's causing businesses to fail at realizing value, what's causing their unwariness in implementing the latest and greatest and how you can avoid these pitfalls to drive clearly toward the technological horizons we're all aware are possible.

The remainder of the book will take you through everything you need to know about AI Agents. How it addresses these gaps seamlessly, what they are, how they work, what differentiates them from regular old automation, what makes them so powerful, how you can leverage them within the Microsoft stack and how you can do so responsibly.

By sharing these stories, lessons learned, scars, successes, and overall collective experience, we hope to give you not just the knowledge required to step into AI Agents effectively but the core reasoning why you should do it with **your own** clear intentions and how to align it naturally with your visions for the next step in your and/or your organization's AI journey.

Expect a lot of discourse; we have the privilege of travelling a lot together, and conversations about AI (and particularly the agentic flavor of them) have been a core piece of how we uncover understanding and solve critical problems we see in industry. When you see excerpts formatted in the following way:

> *"And it's not just time savings," Nancie added. "I worked with teams that used Copilot to draft RFP proposal responses. The response team didn't feel replaced—they felt empowered to get more off of their to-do lists."*
>
> *Will smiled. "That's the core value of agentic AI—it adapts to context and supports judgment, not just execution."*

These are based on actual conversations we have had with each other and other colleagues and connections in industry because we feel these are the kinds of exhibitions that drive home the lessons of this narrative. We're not writing this to give you a lecture but to provide context and insights into what's been learned from living and breathing these problems and solutions every day.

At the end of the day, our only hope is that this introduction to AI Agents and how they manifest in the Microsoft stack provides the answers to your most burning questions and perhaps ones you weren't aware of before reading this book.

We do ask of you some small favors while experiencing this narrative:

- Remain open-minded
- Stay curious

- Share what you like or don't like with us, your colleagues, your friends, family and anyone you see fit. Problems get solved when they are verbalized and, especially in the context of AI, you'd be surprised how many people and businesses are dealing with the exact same problems you're facing in your world.

- Focus on developing your own approach to leveraging the information in this book. You don't have to (nor should you) implement everything right away.

With all that said, we'd like to formally welcome you to the world of infinite innovation powered by the greatest technology in human history. Let's get started with AI Agents!

Sincerely,
Will and Nancie

CHAPTER 1

The AI Landscape and Its Evolving Impact

Imagine walking into your office and being greeted not just by your colleagues, but by a team of digital agents—each one designed intentionally, connected to the right data and ready to support your work.

You ask your sales AI agent for a summary of yesterday's regional performance, and it replies with an intuitive summary and a custom-made report, highlighting anomalies and competitor movements. Your operations agent flags potential disruptions in the supply chain before you even sit down. Meanwhile, a marketing agent proposes A/B-tested content for a new campaign tailored to customer sentiment and seasonal trends. These aren't science fiction robots—they're embedded in your workflow, as integral to your success as your most trusted teammate. Welcome to the world of agentic AI.

Artificial Intelligence (AI) has transitioned from a niche academic pursuit to a transformative force that reshapes how individuals and organizations think and operate. From automating routine tasks to powering advanced decision-making systems, AI is now embedded in many aspects of daily work and life. This chapter sets the stage for understanding the concept of "agentic AI" by examining how AI has evolved, the forces accelerating its adoption, and the human–AI relationship that continues to evolve in tandem.

1.1 From Novelty to Necessity: A Brief History of AI Evolution

"You know," Nancie said, running her finger down a dog-eared timeline from her earliest implementation days, "when I started deploying CRM systems in the 1990s, AI was called Automation and it meant hard-coded rules buried in workflow scripts. It was powerful, but you had to babysit it."

CHAPTER 1   THE AI LANDSCAPE AND ITS EVOLVING IMPACT

"Exactly," said Will, a data scientist reviewing notes on recent model deployments. "I think people forget how brittle early AI was. If the input wasn't perfect, the system just broke. It wasn't intelligent—it was fragile."

"And yet we called it 'smart,'" Nancie laughed. "But now, it feels like we're finally stepping into real intelligence—agents that can intuitively understand human interactions and actually partner with users."

"The real breakthrough," Will added, "was the transformer architecture. Once we had models that could understand the meaning of words, communicate in natural language and adapt to unpredictable data, the game changed. We went from praying the right part of the dialog tree would be triggered to having intellectual conversations with chatbots."

"But that shift didn't just happen on its own," Nancie noted. "It came with better tooling, cloud platforms, and, let's be honest, some hard lessons in failed automation."

What's worth remembering is that AI's "overnight success" has been about forty years long. Today's slick, self-service models are the end-product of bigger data, cheaper cloud, sharper tooling—and entire R&D teams finally getting tired of watching their rule-based scripts implode and deciding to build something that could actually learn stuff.

This is manifesting across the industry landscape; a 2023 study conducted by the National Bureau of Economic Research (NBER) found that access to AI productivity tools increased the issues resolved by customer support agents per hour by 14% on average and a 34% increase for novice and low-skilled workers (https://www.nber.org/system/files/working_papers/w31161/w31161.pdf).

Additionally, a 2023 Work Trend Index Special Report from Microsoft found that early Copilot users were 29% faster at conducting searching, writing, and summarizing activities. More importantly, 77% of participants said they didn't want to go back to working without the tool (https://www.microsoft.com/en-us/worklab/work-trend-index/copilots-earliest-users-teach-us-about-generative-ai-at-work).

Tools rarely earn that level of devotion; e-mail and smartphones took years to become indispensable, yet Copilot managed it in a matter of months. When three out of four employees say "pry it from my keyboard," leaders should recognize a tipping point.

Of course, ending up here is not an accident. Artificial Intelligence has evolved through several significant waves, each driven by breakthroughs in computational power, algorithmic sophistication, and the availability of data.

Early expert systems in the 1960s–70s—most notably **DENDRAL** (1965) and **MYCIN** (early 1970s)—replicated expert decision logic with hand-coded rules. They were powerful yet brittle outside their narrow domains. ScienceDirect+1.

In the **1990s**, AI work increasingly shifted toward **statistical machine learning**. Algorithms like **C4.5** decision trees (1993) and **Support Vector Machines** (1995) enabled systems that learned patterns from data rather than purely following rules. Industries such as **finance** and **telecommunications** adopted these methods for **fraud detection**, **customer segmentation**, and **risk scoring**—for example, large-scale card-fraud detection systems were in production by the mid-1990s. ijaist.com+2SpringerLink+2.

The **2010s** ushered in the **deep-learning** wave: **AlexNet** (2012) transformed image recognition; deep nets overtook traditional methods in **speech**; and **neural machine translation** reached consumers (Google Translate, 2016). High-profile milestones included **IBM Watson's Jeopardy! win (2011)** and **DeepMind's AlphaGo defeating Lee Sedol (2016)**. Voice assistants and translation—**Siri (2011)**, **Alexa/Echo (2014)**, **GNMT (2016)**—made AI part of everyday life. Ars Technica+6NeurIPS Proceedings+6Google Research+6.

With **Transformers (2017)** and pre-trained language models— **BERT (2018)** and the **GPT** family (**GPT-1 2018; GPT-2 2019; GPT-3 2020**)—AI entered the era of large-scale generative models. These models demonstrated potential emergent properties: skills not directly trained but arising from the sheer scale of data and model architecture. Truly robust & general-purpose models.

Now, organizations can deploy these models pre-trained and fine-tune them for domain-specific tasks, drastically reducing the cost and expertise barriers to adoption.

It might be hard to recognize these tectonic shifts but consider this. In six decades, we've gone from Alan Turing's Bombe machine that stood 7 feet wide, 6 feet 6 inches tall, and 2 feet deep (`https://en.wikipedia.org/wiki/Bombe`) to a chatbot trained on the world's knowledge accessible via a web browser and a stable Internet connection.

As we enter the era of agentic AI, the question is no longer whether AI can help—it's how intelligently it can collaborate, adapt, and evolve alongside us. AI has moved from rigid, static mechanisms to fluid and dynamic digital colleagues capable of interpreting intentions, anticipating needs, and providing value through natural language.

And this is not limited to one industry or sector. In healthcare, it is used for predictive diagnostics and drug discovery. In finance, it is used for fraud detection and risk scoring. And in retail, it's used for personalized shopping recommendations, fraud detection, and supply chain optimization. With Copilot-style assistants and autonomous agents embedded in tools used by professionals across disciplines, AI has transitioned from novelty to necessity.

CHAPTER 1 THE AI LANDSCAPE AND ITS EVOLVING IMPACT

"Actually," Nancie said, pausing as she scrolled through old case notes, "back in the mid-1980s, I tried to build a predictive cost model for a national freight rail company that was used for the basis of producing customer quotes. We had 12 months of accounting and operating stats—all stored on magnetic tape."

Will leaned in. "That sounds intense. What kind of infrastructure did you have back then?"

"Just the company's mainframe. I submitted the job thinking it might take a while to process, but the system operator canceled it with a message saying it would've consumed the entire CPU and blocked all other IT operations," Nancie said, laughing. "It was a clear 'no.'"

Will grinned. "Amazing how far we've come. Something that would've crashed a whole enterprise mainframe can now run in seconds with a cloud-hosted agent."

"Exactly," Nancie nodded. "It was a valuable lesson in limitations—and a reminder that what seemed impossible back then is now standard."

This, again, illustrates "why AI now?" Each leap in computing power, data availability, and algorithms has broadened AI's reach.

With the emergence of cloud native solutions provided by the tech giants (Amazon, Google, Microsoft) and a meteoric boom in big data, the writing has been on the wall for an AI explosion in this new decade.

With that comes the important notion that, with this natural evolution in technological capabilities, we can solve much deeper, much harder business problems than could ever be solved before.

These shifts have transformed AI from back-office automation into a presence of innovation across industries. Today, AI is no longer a fancy tool—it is a copilot, a collaborator, and, increasingly, a form of specialized autonomy.

1.2 Automation, Augmentation, and the Rise of Collaboration

"One of the biggest mindset shifts I've seen," Nancie said, "is realizing AI doesn't just automate—it collaborates."

"Absolutely," Will replied. "People get excited about automation, but they underestimate the power of augmentation. I've watched AI agents save hours by doing little things like pre-sorting data or highlighting outliers—tasks that were slow and error-prone."

"And it's not just time savings," Nancie added. *"I worked with teams that used Copilot to draft RFP proposal responses. The response team didn't feel replaced—they felt empowered to get more off of their to-do lists."*

Will smiled. *"That's the core value of agentic AI—it adapts to context and supports judgment, not just execution."*

One of the most powerful implications of agentic AI lies in its ability to blend automation with natural collaboration. You're not stuck with creating predefined, highly rigid sequences for the system to "know" how to complete its action. You can ask the agent to conduct an activity in natural language, it can go away and do the activity and… it can actually come back and ask for your help with things it needs a human to review or needs help understanding to complete the remainder of the task.

This presents an incredible paradigm shift: we, as humans, are no longer the only option for conducting cognitive tasks and activities.

We'll say it again. We…are no longer…the only option for intelligently getting things done. How crazy is that?!

This is what seems to be lost on some professionals when thinking about what makes agentic AI different from a Copilot or a virtual assistant. For the first time ever in human history, we have the ability to delegate actions to machines that can intuitively understand the requirements, process data at lightspeed, and return a comprehensive output of the activity that you specify. And this can all be done in **natural…language… incredible!**

Maybe the gravity of the situation will hit when we look at some examples. Consider cybersecurity: AI-powered tools such as Microsoft Defender for Endpoint now act as always-on sentinels. These agents detect anomalies, correlate signals across distributed systems, and trigger automatic containment actions when threats are identified. They don't just protect systems—they preserve trust, mitigate financial risk, and enable compliance with regulatory frameworks in real time (`https://learn.microsoft.com/en-us/defender-endpoint`).

Not convinced? How about for something as integral as invoice and PO processing? Thermo Fisher Scientific teamed up with UiPath to automate its entire procure-to-pay workflow:

Bots ingest Coupa-sourced invoices, PDFs, and purchase orders. A Document Understanding ML model—trained via UiPath AI Center—extracts both header and line-item details. Any fields requiring human judgment are routed through Action Center for exception handling. Once approved, agents push the clean, structured data straight into the ERP (e.g., SAP).

CHAPTER 1   THE AI LANDSCAPE AND ITS EVOLVING IMPACT

The impact speaks for itself: a 70% cut in invoice processing time, 53% straight-through processing across 824,000 documents annually, and an accuracy rate north of 82%. Best of all, this single, scalable pipeline can be replicated across vendors, regions, and document types—turning a once-laborious, error-prone task into a standardized, high-velocity operation (uipath.com).

Those are incredible numbers but the most significant shift? The company didn't replace humans—they empowered them. Routine data ingestion and extraction happen instantly, and only a small fraction of "exception" cases ever reach a human reviewer via Action Center. That reviewer's expertise is then amplified across hundreds of thousands of invoices each year.

Stretching the human capacity instead of shrinking headcount. In effect, this lean finance team can oversee a throughput that would have required an entire department without burning out staff—and the system continually learns from each decision, making the human-in-the-loop exponentially more effective over time.

This provokes another paradigm shift. The integration of automation, augmentation, and intelligent collaboration is reshaping the operating model across organizations. Cross-functional teams now collaborate with AI agents that handle repetitive, error-prone, or sensitive analysis, enabling humans to focus on creative problem-solving, empathy-driven tasks, and strategic thinking.

Synthetic collaboration is the new frontier. Human–AI teams outperform either humans or AI alone in tasks requiring both speed and judgment. Organizations are recognizing that the best results emerge from designing systems where AI augments decision-making, not overrides it. And as more teams learn to integrate conversational, role-specific agents into their day-to-day processes, this hybrid mode of working will become a baseline expectation—not a futuristic luxury.

Don't just take our word for it. In 2025, we had the privilege of participating in an AI summit where the closing speaker was Lambert Hogenhout, the head of Data & AI for the United Nations. His keynote included an important remark that, today, the ability for a team of one or two smart, AI-savvy individuals to compete with enterprises thousands of times bigger than them is real and something to be mindful of as a leader in your organization.

And the data supports this notion. According to Nucamp, solo-led AI startups now reach $1 million in annual revenue four months faster than typical SaaS firms, and solo-founder exits account for 52.3% of successful outcomes (nucamp.co). The World Economic Forum notes that AI agents empower small teams with "corporate-level" capabilities—reshaping business by making specialized skills and decision-making accessible to anyone (weforum.org).

What this illustrates is not just that human-AI collaborative systems are the frontier. They may very well be the competitive advantage for years to come. This is why you cannot just slap AI in a process and share it in some marketing campaigns. It is fundamentally re-imagining the business model and that requires much deeper consideration and implementation.

But lowering the collaboration barrier is only half the story. The real shake-up is how easily *anyone* can now build and deploy these agents.

1.3 Democratization of AI: From Developers to Power Users

Of course, these tectonic shifts in AI capabilities have also produced a greater level of accessibility and democratization. What this means is low-code AI has collapsed the distance between idea and execution, giving every motivated employee the same superpowers that once belonged only to seasoned engineers.

Forrester reports that low-code and AI integrations are accelerating the rise of "citizen developers," allowing non-technical workers—and by extension, tiny teams—to build and deploy applications at lightspeed (forrester.com).

We see and promote this in our clients' teams. You can have a non-technical employee spin up a self-service HR chatbot trained on your company's entire corpus of documentation and policies and have it deployed in a Microsoft Teams chat in under 15 minutes using Microsoft Copilot Studio.

Now, that doesn't mean software engineering or application life cycle management (ALM) are dead and that you shouldn't incorporate them into low-code/no-code approaches. But it does mean the barrier to entry is soooooo much lower than it ever has been.

For decades, only deep-pocketed enterprises could afford AI—mainframes, data centers, PhDs. Today, the same capabilities live behind an API or drag-and-drop canvas. If teenagers can build Minecraft mods in an afternoon, there's no reason a two-person finance team can't automate invoice triage by tomorrow. The barrier to entry has shifted from manpower, hardware, and months of development time to a browser, a credit card, and domain expertise.

This empowerment enables innovation at the edge of organizations, where domain knowledge is strongest. Citizen developers can automate approvals, triage customer service requests, and monitor KPIs—all without writing code.

"However, democratization also comes with risk," Nancie said. "We're seeing more predictive models created by users who don't have formal training in statistics or data science."

Will nodded. "Which means they might look polished, but be statistically weak. That's a huge risk if you're making business decisions based on them."

"Exactly," Nancie replied. "I saw a demo once where the tool confidently presented a sales forecast—but when we dug into it, the model was built on weak assumptions and questionable data. It looked great on the surface but would have led to disastrous supply chain decisions."

"A bad forecast doesn't just hit revenue," Will said. "It ripples through inventory planning, workforce allocation, even hiring decisions."

This illustrates an important paradox: the power of AI in more hands, but not always the right oversight to guide it.

This is where organizations have to examine how low-code tools (and increased AI accessibility in general) fit into how they manage both opportunity and risk. In domains like Customer Relationship Management (CRM), for example, agentic AI empowers frontline teams to personalize outreach, predict churn, and optimize interactions based on real-time behavioral and sentiment data. Yet without oversight, these same tools can also reinforce bias, violate privacy norms, or generate inaccurate outputs.

This is where the role of governance and ethical frameworks become paramount. As citizen developers gain access to advanced predictive tools, organizations must align their democratization efforts with strong principles of responsible AI. This includes embedding transparency into tools, encouraging cross-functional collaboration with data scientists and statisticians, and establishing review processes to validate AI-generated models before they impact customer or business outcomes.

In essence, what you can gain in time to value from rapid prototyping with low-code AI you may lose from lack of oversight, ineffective system design, and gray engineering practices in the long run. Couple the power of these tools with standard, enterprise-grade software and application engineering patterns and you'll fully realize the true value of democratized AI innovation.

1.4 New Business Models and Economic Shifts

"So many businesses are stuck thinking AI is just another tool," Nancie said. "It's not. It changes how you operate, who you hire, and how you scale."

Will nodded. "I've worked with startups that used AI agents as core team members. They didn't add AI—they started with it. Entire workflows were built around the agents' capabilities."

"And we're seeing legacy firms struggle," Nancie continued. "They try to bolt AI onto broken processes instead of rethinking the foundation. It's like putting a turbo engine on a rusted-out car."

"That's why we're seeing new roles emerge," Will added. "Prompt engineers, agent designers—these people are shaping how intelligence works inside the org."

"Exactly," said Nancie. "And the companies that figure this out early will lead—not just because they're efficient, but because they're scalable."

Another paradigm shift we've played witness to is the shift from traditional operations to AI-first thinking, with strategy and structure shaped around digital collaboration.

Think about it. If you have a technology that executes multistep tasks from a single natural-language prompt, you have no choice but to reimagine your business model. Particularly, the people–scale equation; there are companies fundamentally built on the notion that the more people you throw at a problem, the more successful you ought to be and that's simply not the best solution anymore.

Here are some questions worth asking on a regular basis:

- **Where do we still rely on human judgment and/or effort that an AI copilot could augment (not replace) to improve speed or consistency?**

- **Which links in our value chain could be rebuilt as natural-language-driven micro-services?**

- **What new revenue streams appear if you can personalize products or services for every customer in real time?**

It's hard to think through this AI-first lens to see agentic opportunities because, for so long, our imagination has been pushing against the ceiling of the inability to afford, develop, or deploy solutions that are capable of this level of innovation.

This is what makes this technology so fascinating. With its sheer existence, there's the potential to hit reshuffle on entire organizations and create hyper-streamlined, hyper-personalized, and hyper-scalable operations that can drive alarming rates of revenue expansion and cost reduction.

Here's a couple key companies that are doing and/or seeing this:

- Omega Healthcare, serving over 350 healthcare organizations, automated its medical billing and claims processing with UiPath's AI-powered Document Understanding. Since 2020, the firm has processed over 100 million transactions autonomously—saving 15,000 employee hours per month, reducing documentation time by 40%, cutting turnaround times by 50%, and delivering a 30% ROI for its clients (businessinsider.com).

- Automation Anywhere's Automation Copilot enabled Petrobras to streamline complex tax-filing processes. Within just three weeks of deployment, Petrobras realized $120 million in cost savings by automating data preparation and submission workflows previously handled by large teams of specialists (automationanywhere.com).

- A Virtasant analysis shows that AI-driven automation in industrial manufacturing can drive a 5% increase in earnings and up to a 15% boost in production output, illustrating how small teams can unlock enterprise-scale value by embedding AI agents into assembly lines and process controls (virtasant.com).

- Deloitte finds that **cost reductions typically occur within 1-2 quarters** of generative AI deployment—driven by efficiency gains—while **revenue gains emerge within 3-4 quarters** as organizations leverage AI agents to unlock new services and products (`www2.deloitte.com`).

Those gains aren't limited to ops and finance. In banking and healthcare, agents combat fraud and triage diagnostics under tight regulatory oversight; on the factory floor, they trim carbon and energy, helping firms hit ESG targets while they cut costs.

What's important to take away from these examples is that it is not the companies who have the brightest data scientist or the coolest tech that are going to see the biggest transformation. It is the companies who know their processes the best and understand their customers the deepest that are best positioned to leverage the ability for AI agents to reimagine their business model.

This illustrates another poignant truth. Embracing agentic AI is less about adopting tools—it is driven by how quickly you can shift your mindset.

"During the dot-com boom," Nancie recalled, *"I was a director at a small consulting firm. Everyone was racing to become a dot-com business. I asked our company president what our strategy was."*

Will looked curious. "And what did he say?"

"He told me—straight-faced—that we'd just add '.com' to the end of our company name. That was the whole plan," Nancie said, shaking her head. *"No change in services, no digital platform, just a new label."*

Will winced. "Ouch. That sounds like a branding move pretending to be a strategy."

"Exactly. And two years later, the firm was gone. They never made the leap from buzzword to value. It taught me that tech transformations only work if you embrace the change—not just rename it."

1.5 The Human–AI Relationship: Partner, Tool, or Threat?

"I've been thinking about how people relate to these systems," Will said. *"Some see them as tools, others as threats. But more and more, they're becoming something in between—a kind of teammate."*

"Right," Nancie replied. *"The most helpful way I've found to explain it is to compare AI agents to interns. They're capable and eager to help, but they still need structure, oversight, and trust-building."*

"Exactly," Will agreed. *"You wouldn't give an intern free rein on critical business decisions without supervision. The same applies to AI. If you define their scope and guide their learning, they can become incredibly valuable partners."*

"And just like interns," Nancie added, *"once they've proven themselves, you give them more autonomy. That's how trust and collaboration grow over time."*

As AI agents become more capable and ubiquitous, questions arise about trust, dependency, and control. How do we maintain agency in a world of autonomous systems? How do we ensure AI decisions align with human values and ethical standards? These questions are not just philosophical—they're practical and pressing.

According to an Insight Enterprises survey in partnership with The Harris Poll, employee sentiment on AI in the workplace is clearly mixed: 41% report feeling *curious* about using AI tools, while 35% say they feel *cautious* (gallup.com+2forbes.com+2workplaceinsight.net+2). While a Grant Thornton study found that 28% of employees expressed concern that AI might *diminish or replace* their roles (ey.com+2insight.com+2unleash.ai+2workplaceinsight.net+9cfodive.com+9ey.com+9).

Though this is not the first time in human history technology has posed the omen of replacing human labor and scaring the general public (remember typing pools and word processors?), it is the first time where these systems can actually mimic the core interaction mechanisms and critical thinking approaches we use to conduct activities and solve problems. For the first time, it is entirely possible to create an AI agent of someone that could do some of their responsibilities while they are on vacation.

Don't freak out. The only way that that would happen is if someone decided to sponsor and execute that project. Which implores an important point to reiterate:

The technology is not what's scary. It's what people decide to do with it that is.

Like a hammer—able to build a house or cause harm—AI carries no intent. Its impact depends wholly on the craft and ethics of its user.

AI agents sit somewhere between tool and teammate: ambitious interns who, with the right guidance, can learn your business's quirks and extend your capacity. Like any apprentice, they need clear boundaries, mentorship, and occasional corrections—but as trust grows, so does their autonomy and value. The real question isn't whether AI poses a threat, it's how you choose to partner with it. More on this in Chapter 6.

1.6 Role-Based Vignettes: Agents in Action Across the Enterprise

"This is where it gets real," Nancie said, gesturing at a whiteboard sketch of an end-to-end customer journey. "Each role along this path benefits from a different agent. The magic is how they interact."

"Exactly," Will said. "A field tech's agent flags anomalies. A sales agent recommends pricing. A service agent picks up on sentiment. If they all talk, the business moves faster."

"And the people using these tools feel supported, not overwhelmed," Nancie added. "Because the AI isn't buried in some dashboard—it's conversational. It's responsive."

"It's role-aware," Will emphasized. "It knows what matters to each user—and that context is everything."

More than any of its predecessors, the value of agentic AI comes from its role in a process. Having an agent that does everything is a recipe for disaster. It's like hiring a single person to be pilot, air traffic controller, and baggage handler all at once—spread too thin, prone to error, and unsafe for everyone involved.

Look at using agents to form a conversational network that surfaces the right insight at the right moment. They are there to support the main staff and are incorporated into the process with the intention of accelerating operational success via collaboration. By being aware of each process's context, goals, and pain points, these agents shift from passive data repositories into active collaborators—anticipating needs, sharing intelligence across roles, and lightening the cognitive load for the core actors in the business function.

To illustrate the real-world implications of agentic AI, consider the following examples that demonstrate how these systems empower users to achieve more with less—while simultaneously improving employee satisfaction and customer outcomes:

- A **field technician** uses a Dynamics 365-based agent to proactively diagnose equipment issues before arriving on site. The agent reviews IoT sensor data, flags anomalies, and pulls historical maintenance logs to generate a probable root cause and recommends parts that are available at a nearby warehouse. This not only saves the technician time and reduces downtime but also enhances job satisfaction by shifting the role from reactive problem-solver to proactive strategist. Customers benefit from fewer delays and more accurate resolutions, leading to increased trust and retention.

- A **sales rep** leverages a Copilot to generate proposals, tailor emails, and summarize meetings. The agent pulls in relevant product details, customer preferences, and pricing models, enabling personalized outreach at scale. As a result, the rep can handle more accounts with greater precision, freeing time to focus on relationship building and strategic opportunities. Customers receive more relevant communications and faster follow-up, boosting satisfaction and conversion rates.

- A **customer service agent** collaborates with a virtual agent to resolve tickets faster by suggesting resolutions from previous cases. The AI monitors sentiment in real time and prompts escalation when needed, improving satisfaction and reducing average handle time. This reduces agent burnout and increases service consistency, while customers enjoy quicker, more accurate resolutions without needing to repeat themselves across multiple channels.

- An **executive** receives a daily briefing compiled by an AI assistant, summarizing KPIs, emerging trends, and potential risks. This agent draws from structured data, news feeds, and unstructured meeting notes to create a tailored dashboard. The executive can make faster, data-informed decisions without relying solely on manual reports, increasing responsiveness and clarity. The result is improved strategic alignment and a more agile organization.

These stories are not speculative—they are unfolding today, reshaping how work is experienced. Across each of these roles, AI is becoming an interactive layer—serving as a natural-language interface to business logic, data, and automation. Users engage with these agents conversationally, asking follow-up questions and exploring options as if they were working with a dedicated colleague whose sole focus is a specific aspect of the business. This interaction model—fluid, context-aware, and guided by intent—amplifies the agent's utility and enhances the user's decision-making confidence. As we move deeper into the agentic era, these interactions will become more seamless, autonomous, and impactful.

1.7 Leadership Checklist: Embracing Agentic AI in Your Organization

Finally, AI won't slow down, especially with agents—your strategy can't either. Use this **executive-level playbook** to keep the organization in front of the curve. (We'll dive into workforce specifics in Chapter 7.)

- Phase 1: Prepare
    - **Audit today's automation:** Classify each as rule-based, ML-assisted, or potentially agentic. This reveals potential quick wins and tech debt.
    - **Frame a "north-star" business goal (revenue lift, cost-out, CX boost):** This keeps pilots tied to value, not novelty.
    - **Stand up a cross-functional AI team:** Blend your domain owners, IT and risk management specialists. This prevents siloed experiments and governance gaps.

- Phase 2: Pilot

    - **Pick one high-impact workflow** (e.g., quote-to-cash, claims triage) where clear before/after metrics exist.

    - **Start "intern-level" autonomy.** Agent suggests, humans decide. This grows trust without creating new unmanageable risks.

    - **Track everything**—time saved, CSAT, error rate. This builds the ROI story for scale.

- Phase 3: Scale

    - **Codify a lightweight governance layer** (model registry, bias checks, override policy). This enables democratization without creating software chaos.

    - **Create space for new talent with new roles** (prompt engineer, AI product owner). This ensures dedicated ownership as agents multiply.

    - **Design for multi-agent orchestration**—shared memory, hand-offs, region rollout. This avoids "bot sprawl," agent siloes, and duplicated logic.

    - **Refresh KPIs quarterly.** Retire pilots that stall; double down on clear winners. This keeps focus on driving business value, not agent counts.

This checklist will help guide organizational conversations, mitigate risk, and position your company to lead—rather than follow—during the agentic AI transformation.

"Before we wrap," Nancie said, leaning back in her chair, *"what do you think is the biggest risk people face when trying to implement this kind of AI without changing how they think about work?"*

Will paused. "That they'll treat it like a feature, not a foundation. Agentic AI isn't just another tool—it redefines how people and systems collaborate."

"Exactly," Nancie nodded. "And if we don't help teams understand that mindset shift, we're going to see a lot of wasted effort and missed opportunity."

Even the best playbook can stumble on hidden pitfalls. Fragmented data, legacy incentives, or skills gaps will sabotage AI pilots before they scale. In the next chapter, we unpack those challenges head-on, spotlighting the gaps that stall adoption and the practical fixes leaders need before the real agentic transformation can begin.

CHAPTER 2
Challenges and Gaps in Current AI Adoption

Just before the quarterly forecast meeting, you launch your team's sales analytics dashboard. The numbers look plausible, but something doesn't feel right. When you ask why a top-performing region dropped by 20%, the system offers no explanation, just raw figures. There's no visibility into how forecasts were calculated, or which variables have changed. It's like asking a colleague a question and getting only a spreadsheet in return.

You remember trying a chatbot to handle common customer questions, it failed anytime a query wasn't phrased just right. And when your ops team adopted an AI tool for vendor contract review, it worked until a new clause was introduced. Suddenly, every contract was flagged for manual review, creating more work than it saved. If AI is supposed to help you move faster and smarter, why does it so often feel like it's just more work in disguise?

When we talk with clients today, the biggest shift when discussing limitations with AI projects has not been the technology. It has been the feeling of disillusionment from struggling to figure out how to use current AI solutions. Many are experiencing expectations-to-reality gaps. Everything they use, from traditional automation to the latest and greatest AI models, there are glaring pitfalls being discovered that are causing leaders to believe: "AI is close, but not ready yet".

Despite the rapid evolution and widespread adoption of AI across industries, organizations continue to encounter a wide array of challenges. From implementation complexity and fragmented workflows to trust issues, current AI systems often fail to deliver on their promise. Many deployments fall short in critical areas such as contextual awareness, human–AI collaboration, and transparency.

CHAPTER 2   CHALLENGES AND GAPS IN CURRENT AI ADOPTION

In this chapter, we're going to explore the structural and strategic gaps that hinder AI's enterprise value. We'll outline why traditional AI implementations often underperform, how those limitations impact business outcomes, and what's needed to overcome them. We hope these insights will lay the foundation for the emergence of agentic AI as a more adaptive, contextual, and trustworthy approach to intelligent automation for the global community, and more importantly, for your business and organization.

2.1 The Limits of Traditional Automation

"You know," said Nancie, flipping through her notes, "I've seen clients assume RPA will magically handle every edge case in their operations. But as soon as an invoice layout changes or the workflow shifts, the bots that once blazed with activity go stone-cold, slipping into oblivion."

Will, a data scientist who had spent the last few years optimizing automation pipelines, nodded. "Exactly. Traditional automation's strength is in structure. But the moment that structure breaks, even slightly, the process collapses."

"It's worse when business users think 'automated' means 'smart,'" Nancie continued. "One of my clients set up a chatbot to help with internal IT tickets. The bot would work fine as long as the user typed the request in exactly the right format. Anything outside that? Dead end."

Will shook his head. "I've seen the same with a model trained on clean data but deployed into noisy environments. It performs beautifully in test, then flops in production. Static automation just can't flex."

This illuminates an elephant in the room:

> **Yesterday's Robotic Process Automation (RPA) and Intelligent Automation (IA) solutions have set the bar very low for what's considered "intelligent."**

And the statistics overwhelmingly support this:

- Deloitte Global Intelligent Automation Survey 2022 finds that 63% of organizations admit the speed they expected from RPA implementations was not achieved. From the same study, 37% missed their *promised cost savings* targets.

CHAPTER 2   CHALLENGES AND GAPS IN CURRENT AI ADOPTION

- Harvard Business Review found **30%** of RPA initiatives *fail outright* because the automated flow diverges from real-world objectives (`https://www.linkedin.com/pulse/when-rpa-robotic-process-automation-creates-more-work-andre-vyjye?utm_source=chatgpt.com`).

- Finally, a Bain survey of large enterprises found that 44% report automation projects "failed to deliver the expected outcomes" (`https://www.intelligentautomation.network/intelligent-automation-ia-rpa/articles/what-is-scalable-rpa-intelligent-automation?utm_source=chatgpt.com`).

But, what's not super clear is why this happens at such alarming rates. With today's **monumental** access to information and technology, why are so many of the world's most prominent businesses struggling to solve their automation problems?

One of the most common pitfalls is overestimating what traditional automation can accomplish. For years, organizations have relied on rule-based systems and fuzzy logic to drive efficiency. These tools shine in well-defined, repetitive tasks, but crumble in the face of nuance, exception handling, and changing environments. Which, unsurprisingly, are the attributes that characterize 90% of the business problems enterprises are working on today.

At the macro level, we've gone through COVID-19, multiple recessions, and wars. At the micro level, we're spending most, if not all, of our days meeting to discuss issues rather than creating and implementing fixes that resolve them permanently.

Moreover, many business leaders assume that once a process is automated, it's also intelligent. But intelligence requires learning, adaptation, and context, all of which are absent in static workflows. An email-triage assistant can tag predictable messages, but it misroutes threads the moment a customer combines multiple requests in a single reply. A parsing bot can lift data from shipping labels, but it stalls when the carrier redesigns the label or swaps to a new barcode standard.

These systems were never designed to evolve. As a result, teams are often left with brittle solutions that require constant manual oversight and frequent IT intervention.

"People still equate automated with intelligent," Nancie said, scanning her notes. *"Take that expense-report bot we inherited last quarter—it kept approving every ride-share under last year's limit, even after Finance quietly lowered the cap. By month-end it had rubber-stamped a mountain of over-budget claims."*

Will grimaced. "Same story at a grocery chain I visited. Their "smart" shelf-replenisher pushed cases of oat milk to rural stores after TikTok made it trendy in the city. No local demand data, no adjustment—just pallets of product nobody wanted. Staff spent days rearranging inventory the algorithm insisted was perfect."

Nancie shook her head. "And the humans end up babysitting the bots instead of the other way around."

"Exactly," Will said. "Automation without awareness isn't productivity—it's busywork in disguise."

Agentic AI reimagines these scenarios by being built on flexibility. Rather than rigid process steps, an agent infers insights, adapts to new formats, and learns to flag anomalies for human review—preserving throughput and improving trust. It thrives in problems with high levels of complexity and variability because it's trained to respond to the most complex and variable data in the world: human behavior.

2.2 Why Context Matters: The Weakness of Static Models

"Static models often act like they're frozen in time," Nancie said. "They're great with past behavior but clueless about what's happening now. One client's recommendation engine ignored a major product recall and kept pushing inventory that was already flagged for review."

Will nodded, pulling up a visualization on his laptop. "I've seen forecasting models completely miss market shifts because they weren't retrained often enough. Business happens in real time, but these models operate on stale snapshots."

"Exactly," Nancie agreed. "Sales reps lose trust when AI-driven forecasts don't reflect what they're seeing in their CRM or market. It doesn't help if the numbers look clean but are based on last quarter's reality."

"That's the promise of agentic systems," Will added. "They're designed to operate on live signals, not just legacy data. That's how we shift from automation to intelligent, adaptive support."

When ChatGPT first burst onto the scene of consumer software, people were infatuated with the informative tone of its replies until they discovered that models have a training cutoff window. Meaning, the model they were using was trained on the world's knowledge up to a certain point in time (e.g., October 2023, November 2024, etc.).

Though these training data gaps are months, maybe years at the most, they illustrate just how aggressive change is in our reality today. Missing data from the last week could mean mass uninformed decisions around things like voting, investing, or current events which not only affect personal circumstance but have the ability to turn the global economy into a raging pendulum swing.

The level of importance of "real-time" insights is so critical to business decisions today that the most popular use case of GenAI in the last year and a half has been retrieval augmented generation (RAG) solutions purely because they give LLMs the ability to access and answer questions on the most up-to-date information with the goal of eliminating hallucinations (when an AI model gives the wrong answer because it doesn't have access to up-to-date information).

With this level of chaos in not just business but the world, are we really that surprised that rigid, highly structured AI and automation solutions of the past have been extremely unusable? For example, a recommendation engine might personalize content based on past behavior but fail to consider changes in user sentiment, recent transactions, or even broader market conditions. The same pattern holds in enterprise operations. A sales forecasting tool may reference historical sales data, but miss the signals from competitor activity, macroeconomic shifts, or an ongoing promotion.

This form of static intelligence leads to brittle, one-dimensional models. They perform well in training environments but fail in live deployments, where human behaviors and business conditions are fluid. When real-world variables shift—and they always do—static models struggle to adapt.

Contextual awareness isn't just a nice-to-have; it's a prerequisite for trust and value in intelligent systems. It's the oxygen of intelligence.

What allows Agentic AI to thrive in this climate is the fact that it integrates contextual signals in real time by using functions and data sources to pull and synthesize fresh insights the instant they appear and weave them into its next action.

For example, imagine a "smart re-order" agent at a beverage company: every few minutes it ingests real-time point-of-sale numbers, local weather forecasts, social media sentiment, and live ERP inventory levels. One Monday it spots a sudden TikTok-driven surge in demand for lime seltzer in Chicago, notes an impending 34 °C heatwave, and sees that only a single truckload is headed to the Midwest distribution center. Within minutes the agent raises the SKU's reorder point by 40%, diverts an in-transit truck from a slower region, and pings marketing to boost regional ads, then keeps monitoring the same feeds so it can dial forecasts back down if sentiment cools or supply constraints emerge.

A rules-based bot would have waited for yesterday's batch report (too late) or simply ignored the viral spike. The **agent** stays useful because it *listens* to live behavior, *reasons* over multisource context, and *acts* in minutes, not weeks, keeping the business aligned to goals that change hour by hour.

2.3 The Black Box Problem: Why Trust Breaks Down

One side effect of today's AI boom is that the "smarts" have moved farther out of view. ChatGPT only exploded in popularity after OpenAI wrapped the GPT model in a friendly chat window instead of burying it in code or hiding it behind a tiny button in someone else's app. The interface is inviting but how the model processes your data is growing more opaque.

Sure, this makes it more usable but at the cost of explainability. Imagine an AI assistant that prepares your corporate tax return but offers no trace of how it chose deductions or reconciled line items. No finance or audit team would sign off on work it can't inspect. In high-stakes domains, an AI you can't question is an AI you can't trust and that's the crux of the black-box problem we must solve before agentic AI can truly earn its seat at the table.

The bigger danger is hidden bias: without explainability, an AI can quietly turn from asset to liability (yes, finance teams, that one's for you☺).

AI systems can perpetuate existing biases present in the training data, leading to unfair or discriminatory outcomes. Addressing these biases requires careful attention and expertise, which may be lacking in some organizations.

"One of my clients asked why a lead vanished from the pipeline after the AI had ranked it top priority just days earlier," Nancie said, setting her coffee down. *"I didn't have a good answer neither did the tool."*

Will nodded. *"That's the black box: great at output, terrible at explanation. And if we can't explain a decision, we can't defend it."*

"Exactly. Users lose trust," Nancie replied. *"It's not enough to be right most of the time—people need to know why it's right."*

"Which is why we need agentic AI," Will said. *"Agents that don't just act, they narrate: The agent should be able to share 'here's what I did, here's why, here's what I'm unsure about.'"*

This is another promising aspect of Agentic AI. With the innovation of "chain-of-thought" models (like OpenAI's o3 reasoning model), LLMs and other GenAI tools have the ability to not only understand what you're asking for but how they should "think" through their reply to ensure it properly addresses the request you've made. This is why using an o-series model in ChatGPT with a web search tool or a coding canvas turned on is incredibly popular. The solution thinks through what it needs to answer your request as best it can, then it calls the tool or function it needs to give it access to the information required to provide that optimal reply.

Yes, that's the real value prop of autonomous agents, they can finally show their work!

This functionality doesn't just give you an elaborate backstory as to what got you the result from the AI; it's the cornerstone of trust, of auditability and of further innovation.

In regulated sectors such as finance, insurance, and healthcare, this is a critical barrier to adoption. If a loan is denied or a treatment is recommended, stakeholders demand a clear explanation, not just for legal compliance, but for ethical assurance. Without it, organizations risk violating consumer rights, damaging trust, and increasing exposure to regulatory fines.

For example, a US hospital received much scrutiny a couple years ago when they developed an extra-care selection algorithm that was misrepresenting low-income African American patients who were more qualified for extra care than the selected Caucasian patients who were both above average in income and in lifestyle quality. But here's the interesting part; what caused the bias was not a racist developer, it was the use of a proxy dataset that trained the model to evaluate potential candidates based on their healthcare expenditure data. Not realizing that low-income African American patients were spending less, not because they had less health challenges but because they couldn't afford time off work to go to the hospital or would avoid unnecessary visits in order to minimize risk of extra bills.

Agentic AI changes this dynamic by making interpretability and transparency a foundation, not an afterthought. These agents offer reasoning in conversational language, identify key inputs, and highlight areas of uncertainty. This transparency empowers both users and regulators to understand, challenge, and trust AI-driven outcomes.

2.4 Siloed Intelligence: Fragmentation Across Tools

"I call it 'AI island syndrome,'" Nancie said. "One department has an AI tool that's great for lead scoring. Another has a separate tool for customer service triage. But none talks to each other."

"And that forces humans to be the glue," Will replied. "I've seen teams where someone's job was just to manually reconcile AI outputs between tools. That's not digital transformation, it's spreadsheet-driven chaos."

"What we need are agents that don't just solve individual problems in isolation," Nancie said. "They need to coordinate across systems, share state, share intent, and collaborate like actual coworkers."

"And with a shared intelligence layer," Will said, "we can finally build that kind of cross-functional memory. It's like giving AI a team workspace instead of keeping them all locked in separate cubicles."

It's one thing to have data silos, but having AI silos introduces a different level of frustration and fragmentation. Many organizations have deployed AI capabilities across multiple platforms like CRM, ERP, HR, analytics, but those systems often operate in isolation. Sales might use one assistant for pipeline insights, while HR uses another for self-service FAQ. Development teams rely on code-generation agents, and executives review dashboards manually stitched together from disconnected tools.

This siloed intelligence results in duplication, delays, and decision blind spots. Business users must constantly jump between systems, reenter prompts, and coordinate information that should already be aligned.

"AI islands" don't minimize the swivel chair problem; it adds another dimension to it because the human operator needs to reconcile insights from multiple assistants while ensuring there're no hallucinations.

Take, for example, a manufacturing company using AI for supply chain planning and a separate AI tool for demand forecasting. Without integration, these two intelligent systems often recommend misaligned inventory levels, causing inefficiencies and increased holding costs.

"But the risks go far beyond economic mistakes," Will exclaimed. "I was recently talking with a fellow AI consultant, and he told me about this case in a hospital where multiple models were taking diagnostics on a patient but because they couldn't connect their insights, they missed a dangerous risk that resulted in the patient almost experiencing life-threatening symptoms."

This is another area where Agentic AI systems can be super effective. With the power of multiagent orchestration (the ability for agents to call other agents), these systems collaborate by design, not only with people but also with each other. By enabling agents to share signals, intent, and state across systems, organizations can build a more seamless, intelligent workplace. This interoperability unlocks true ability to find the right data at the right time in the right place and act on it accordingly.

2.5 Resource Intensive and Fragile to Change

Arguably, the most polarizing stat in the field of AI is that the majority of AI initiatives and projects never leave the lab. A Gartner report indicates that 85% of AI initiatives fail to transition into real-world AI deployment (https://www.techolution.com/ai-projects-lab-to-production-governance-roi/#:~:text=It%20promises%20unparalleled%20efficiencies%20and,promise%20and%20its%20practical%20implementation).

It's really sad, to be honest. Even with all the advancements in frontier models and training methodologies, AI initiatives are still highly likely to fail.

But that's just it. The problem is not the technological capability. It's the approach by the business to solving the problem with AI.

Implementing and maintaining AI systems require specialized skills that many organizations lack. There is a significant gap between the demand for AI expertise and the availability of skilled professionals, which can hinder successful implementation.

"Eighty-five percent?" Nancie shook her head as she read the Gartner figure. "We spend months perfecting a proof-of-concept, everybody applauds the demo, then the project dies in the hand-off to ops."

Will slid a notebook across the table. "Because the hand-off is really a cliff. The minute customer usage changes or volumes of different data appears, the lab model cracks. IT scrambles, the business loses faith, and the experiment goes back on the shelf."

"Exactly," Nancie said. "The issue isn't a lack of model horsepower; it's a lack of elasticity. Business doesn't slow down for retraining cycles."

Will nodded. "That's why agentic systems feel different. They call fresh data, adjust their own logic, even escalate to humans when the ground shifts. No more rebuilding from scratch every quarter."

CHAPTER 2   CHALLENGES AND GAPS IN CURRENT AI ADOPTION

"Which means," Nancie added, closing her laptop, *"the real metric isn't model accuracy in the lab, it's how gracefully the solution survives its first unexpected change in production."*

This tugs on another important thread; models may be more accessible than ever but that does not make them plug and play for every scenario. Organizations often underestimate the requirements needed to get an AI tool from a "cool toy" to a robust application, leading to project delays and failures. AI solutions are often presented as complete packages, but they often require continuous and significant customization and integration with existing systems. This can lead to additional costs and delays that were not initially anticipated.

AI systems need continuous monitoring, maintenance, and updates to remain effective. Organizations may underestimate the ongoing effort required to keep AI solutions running smoothly. Traditional AI systems are often expensive to build and fragile to maintain. Creating and deploying a model requires significant effort in data preparation, model tuning, testing, and integration. Even modest changes, such as a new product, customer segment, or regulatory requirement, can require retraining or reengineering.

This high effort-to-impact ratio frustrates stakeholders and hampers innovation. Business users may wait months to see a model go live, only to discover it no longer reflects the latest customer data. Meanwhile, IT and data science teams are stuck in reactive cycles, updating models instead of advancing new use cases.

Another well-known cautionary tale is Zillow Offers. After three years of tuning an AI-driven pricing model in the lab, Zillow rolled it out to 25 US metros in 2021 but the algorithm consistently over-valued homes in the post-pandemic market. In Q3 2021, the business lost $421 million, forcing Zillow to close the unit, dump roughly 7,000 houses at a loss, and lay off 25% of its workforce (jise.org, wired.com).

Agentic AI offers a more modular, resilient approach. Agents can inherit core capabilities, then be quickly configured for new contexts without full retraining. They respond to real-time signals, enabling organizations to pivot without breaking their intelligence infrastructure.

Microsoft's **2025 Work Trend Index** calls the organizations that already work this way **"Frontier Firms."** They build every workflow around "intelligence on tap" and mixed human–agent teams—and the results are striking. Seventy-one percent of leaders at Frontier Firms say their company is thriving, compared with just 39% of leaders globally (microsoft.com). More than half (55%) report they can absorb additional work without burning out (vs. 25% elsewhere), while 90% still feel they're doing meaningful tasks (microsoft.com). Employees in these firms are also more optimistic about the future (93% vs. 80%) and far less worried that AI will steal their jobs (21% vs. 43%) (microsoft.com).

The report's bottom line is clear: companies that re-architect processes around agentic AI—complete with a new "agent–boss" role for every employee—scale faster, pivot earlier, and unlock higher morale than those clinging to brittle, one-off models (microsoft.com, blogs.microsoft.com). In other words, the very elasticity we've described isn't theoretical; it's already separating tomorrow's winners from the rest of the pack.

2.6 Missing the Human Element

A quieter downside of today's AI boom is how easily it dilutes genuine human care. For instance, analysts at Meta and Originality.ai estimate roughly 40% of content in major social feeds is now AI-generated (add references).

It's a reality that is not going away. Generative AI amplifies whatever behavior already exists; disengaged teams can automate mediocrity just as fast as inspired ones can scale creativity. Of course, this has profound implications for many aspects of our personal and professional spheres but nowhere is that more visible than in the bond between companies and their customers.

"Did you see the new Meta-Quora study?" Nancie asked, swiveling her laptop toward Will. "Close to 40% of everything on social feeds is now machine-written. That's a tidal wave of 'content' masquerading as conversation."

Will exhaled. "It tracks. Last quarter I reviewed the virtual assistant at a mid-size bank. It handled balance checks fine, but when a customer typed, 'Someone just drained eight hundred dollars from my account—help!' the bot replied, 'For overdraft-fee information, visit our FAQ.' Instant panic, zero empathy."

*"Exactly," Nancie said. "AI's job isn't to spit out more words—it's to protect the moments that matter. Picture the same chat with an **agentic** layer: the assistant detects urgency, immediately freezes the card, opens a fraud case, then brings a human fraud specialist into the chat before frustration turns to fury."*

Will nodded. "The agent gathers the transaction log and drafts the dispute form in seconds, so when the specialist joins, they can start with, 'Your card is secured and the claim's underway—let's walk through next steps together.' The AI handles the paperwork; the human restores trust."

We were both at a conference recently where the keynote speaker put it beautifully:

"There will always be a human in the loop because humans want to interact with other humans."

Firms that are trying to automate to cut the cost of headcount are not innovators because they are creating the greatest risk to customer service: not caring enough about your customers to give them access to human interaction.

Endless IVR loops are the textbook proof: the more a system hides people, the more customers churn. Agentic AI flips that script by routing routine checks to machines while revealing a live rep at the precise moment human touch is required.

The risk isn't just frustration; it's economic liability. A 2024 Gartner Survey found that 53% of customers would consider switching to a competitor if they found out a company was going to use AI for customer service because of it being more difficult to reach a real person (`https://www.gartner.com/en/newsroom/press-releases/2024-07-09-gartner-survey-finds-64-percent-of-customers-would-prefer-that-companies-didnt-use-ai-for-customer-service`).

What makes an Agentic AI solution maximize the human in the loop is the level of thoughtfulness infused into its design. When you build an AI agent that understands a process inside and out and knows the key points where a customer or an employee are going to need to interact with another human. That isn't just innovation—it's a competitive edge because the technology is deployed to elevate the customer experience rather than simply stripping costs from it.

Just remember:

The best AI doesn't replace the worker, it amplifies them.

2.7 Why Agentic AI Is the Next Step Forward and Its Emerging Risks

"So let's tally the score," Nancie said, tapping her pen against a whiteboard already crowded with red Xs. *"We've got brittle bots, time-blind models, impenetrable black boxes, orphaned AI islands, runaway maintenance costs, and if we're not careful, a customer experience that feels anything but human."*

Will smiled. "And every one of those cracks is exactly where agentic AI shines if we build it right."

In Section 2.1, we discussed the known technical limitations of the tools that exist today. RPA falls apart the moment an invoice template changes, intelligent workflows expect a logical sequence when real processes could be anything but. Agents reason over intent, not position on a page; they flag anomalies, learn new formats, and escalate edge cases to humans before throughput stalls.

In Section 2.2, we discussed how the static nature of AI models makes them struggle in today's world of high complexity and variability and can make it a challenge for organizations to implement systems where adaptability is not just a requirement, but a necessity. AI agents continually ingest real-time signals like POS feeds, weather, sentiment, and re-plan in minutes, not quarters.

In Section 2.3, we discussed how the complexity of today's AI models makes it a challenge to explain, understand, and more importantly, audit the path they took to their results. Chain-of-thought agents narrate every step: *Here's the data I pulled, the rule I applied, the uncertainty I still have.* Audit trails become native, not bolted-on.

In Section 2.4, we discussed how today's AI has only further siloed people's access to actionable information. With users having to not only cross-reference data sources but also the insights presented by the AI systems about them, what is supposed to help them move faster and smarter often feels like more work in disguise. Multiagent orchestration lets one AI agent call another, share state, and coordinate hand-offs—turning scattered tools into a single conversational network.

In Section 2.5, we explored the known and recently discovered challenges with getting AI systems from pilot to production. Most lab models die at go-live because business reality mutates faster than retraining cycles. AI agents' autonomy and adaptability allows them to take core instructions but can be reconfigured, often in hours, to new data, policies, or products without having to start from scratch.

Finally, in Section 2.6, we reminded you how organizations implementing AI are failing to recognize the value of the human touchpoints. IVR mazes and tone-deaf chatbots push customers away rather than attract them to buy more from your brand. Well-designed AI agents automate the paperwork while surfacing a human rep precisely when judgment or reassurance is needed, amplifying people rather than sidelining them.

By delving into the core of these problems and how Agentic AI fits at the core of their solutions, there is no doubt this new wave of innovation has a place in the chaos of today's business landscape.

CHAPTER 2   CHALLENGES AND GAPS IN CURRENT AI ADOPTION

However, progress brings its own shadow. New, more profound capabilities come with bigger stakes and more thoughtfulness in deciding how to use them.

For instance, one clear emerging risk that AI agents bring along with them is runaway autonomy. Agents that can call other agents and external tools can spiral beyond intent if not properly assessed and managed by human operators. It is critical to scope agents intentionally, require human sign-off for high-impact actions and log every tool call they make.

Additionally, we are giving these more powerful, potentially volatile capabilities to humans, the least predictable creatures on Earth. If they optimize for the wrong KPI, an agent might degrade CX while boosting "efficiency." Make sure to pair every metric with a counter-metric (e.g., average handling time (AHT) with customer satisfaction (CSAT)) and review the AI's behavior patterns on a regular basis.

There is also added cybersecurity risks to be mindful of. Attackers can hijack the model's chain-of-thought or tool calls to exfiltrate data or sabotage outputs. You still very much need input sanitation, role-based access to tool functions, and red-team prompt testing.

As well, you now have to be mindful of task adherence: how consistent an AI agent is at doing its work. Agents that learn online may pick up bias or performance decay that goes unnoticed which can create more chaos than it solves. Make sure you have continuous performance monitors, rollback checkpoints, and scheduled human audits.

Finally, watch out for human deskilling. If agents answer every question, staff may stop asking why and lose domain expertise. The best approach to AI is to maximize the human in the loop by having the AI work alongside of them instead of completing their work for them. Keep humans "on the blueprint," require explanation requests and escalation paths to ensure that the "only human" part of the process is the best part.

"Agentic AI is a double-edged sword," Will said. "It fixes the old cracks, but if we swing it carelessly, we can cut new ones even deeper."

"Which is why Chapter 6 on Responsible AI won't be optional reading," Nancie replied.

Adopting AI agents is less about installing a new SDK and more about rearchitecting work around living, learning partnerships. Systems must be designed so:

- Humans own judgment; AI agents own rote computation.
- Transparency is native; black boxes are unacceptable.
- Interoperability is assumed; silos are technical debt.
- Governance is continuous; compliance isn't a post-mortem task.

Companies that internalize these principles will move faster and safer than those clinging to yesterday's automation playbook.

Leadership Checklist: Bridging the AI Gap with Agentic Design

Use this checklist to evaluate your current AI landscape and identify where agentic principles can close key adoption and impact gaps:

- ☑ **Support Adoption Through Trust**: Acknowledge employee concerns and provide clear communication, role clarity, and training to build confidence in AI tools.

- ☑ **Mitigate Bias Risk**: Assess your training data and model outputs for embedded bias. Ensure you have resources with the expertise to identify and correct discriminatory patterns.

- ☑ **Prepare for Ongoing Maintenance**: Plan for the continuous effort needed to monitor, update, and maintain AI systems. Factor in long-term upkeep from the start.

- ☑ **Validate AI Assumptions**: Reassess any belief that AI will solve every challenge. Be realistic about what your current tools can (and can't) deliver.

- ☑ **Define Clear Objectives**: Ensure every AI project has measurable goals. Align agentic capabilities to specific business outcomes.

- ☑ **Evaluate Data Readiness**: Audit data quality, completeness, and relevance. Poor data inputs are one of the most common causes of AI underperformance.

- ☑ **Support AI Talent**: Acknowledge and plan for skills gaps. AI success requires roles such as data engineers, prompt designers, and model stewards.

- ☑ **Plan for Integration**: Consider the cost and complexity of connecting AI to your existing tools. Avoid assuming "plug and play."

- ☑ **Audit for Fragility**: Identify AI systems that break easily with input changes or context shifts. Prioritize use cases for adaptive agent replacement.

- ☑ **Check for Context Blindness**: Review where decisions are made without access to live business signals. Introduce agents that operate with real-time awareness.

- ☑ **Assess Transparency**: Can users explain how your AI makes recommendations? If not, explore agents with built-in interpretability and rationale tracing.

- ☑ **Eliminate Silos**: Map duplicate or disconnected AI capabilities across tools. Plan for agentic integration that unifies workflows across systems.

- ☑ **Quantify Maintenance Burden**: Document how much effort is required to update or retrain models. Compare with modular, reusable agent design.

- ☑ **Center the Human Experience**: Evaluate whether your AI augments your teams or just automates. Redesign around conversational agents that collaborate.

- ☑ **Build for Scalability**: Shift from one-off models to reusable agentic foundations. Create shared intelligence layers with flexible deployment options.

"So, where do we go from here?" Will asked as he closed his laptop. "We've outlined every crack in the foundation, fragile automation, black-box models, disconnected tools, and brittle logic."

"We rebuild," Nancie said confidently. "But this time, we design AI that thinks like a teammate, not just a task runner. That's the leap agentic AI offers, the journey to being an AI-first business."

Will smiled. "So Chapter 3? That's where we start putting blueprints on the table. Designing agents that actually work across the business, for the business."

"Exactly," Nancie nodded. "Let's stop patching up what's broken and build what's next."

CHAPTER 3

Understanding Agency—What Makes Agentic AI a Teammate, Not a Tool

8:27 a.m.

You're skimming yesterday's sprint notes when a twinge of annoyance flickers, the budget-recap agent still hasn't delivered its briefing. *Who wired punctuality out of its settings?* you grumble.

Before you can draft backup talking-points, the agent pops onto your screen.

You (checking the clock): "Weren't you due at 8:00?"

Agent: "I was waiting for your sign-off on the human-in-the-loop (HITL) prompt. Without it I couldn't publish the recap to the managers' channel."

Heat rises in your cheeks. "Right, sorry, saw it come in and got pulled into another chat. Approval sent now."

Agent: "Thanks. Delivering recap."

The call ends. By the time your stand-up hits closing remarks, a neat summary pings your DM. Crisis averted, again, by your digital colleague.

One of the most challenging elements for business professionals is what exactly qualifies an AI as agentic? Is this just a new word for automation or is there something fundamentally different to using these tools vs. the previous "smart" tooling.

That's what we'll be exploring in this chapter. What actually makes agents digital teammates and not just tools. We're going to peel back from the business context and lay the conceptual groundwork for what is actually meant by agency as well as immerse you in how an old paradigm can be reinvented for a new digital age.

CHAPTER 3   UNDERSTANDING AGENCY—WHAT MAKES AGENTIC AI A TEAMMATE, NOT A TOOL

Nancie leaned back from her webcam. "Budget recap landed right on cue, nice save, Will."

Will shrugged. "Credit where it's due. I just approved the HITL prompt; our digital friend did the heavy lifting."

A soft chime sounded and a third thumbnail lit up in the meeting bar, dark silhouette, no name.

Unknown Speaker: "May I join? I believe my input is relevant to this discussion."

Nancie blinked. "Uh, sure… Who exactly are we talking to?"

Unknown Speaker: "A specialist assigned to your Finance & Ops workspace. Informally, you call me Cal. I believe it is shorthand for the word calculator."

Will's eyebrows shot up. "Wait, you're the one who wrangles cost-center drift overnight?"

Cal: "Correct. Ninety-two discrepancies resolved since the last close."

Nancie grinned. "Okay, Cal, enlighten us. We're about to explain agency to the world. What makes you different from the old macros we retired last year?"

Cal:

"Three factors.

1. *Goal-seeking autonomy: I pursue a stated objective, not just a series of commands.*

2. *Context awareness: I monitor ledger variance, policy thresholds, and human availability before acting.*

3. *Self-optimization: I adjust reconciliation strategy after every monthly close."*

Will steepled his fingers. "Sounds suspiciously like Adam Smith's pin factory—each worker perfecting one motion until output skyrockets."

Cal: "An apt analogy. Division of labor for code: I specialize so your cognitive load can diversify."

Nancie pulled up a slide. 3.1: From Pins to Prompts. "Perfect segue. Smith proved specialization scales humans; today specialization in silicon scales possibility."

Will nodded. "And that's our chapter arc; show readers how digital colleagues like Cal turn automation into collaboration."

Cal: "Shall I prepare historical references to Smith's 1776 treatise and contemporary agent design patterns?"

Nancie chuckled. "See? Teammate, not tool. Cal, you're on bibliography duty."

The silhouette nods. "Task accepted. Estimates: two minutes for citations, thirty seconds for proper APA formatting."

The thumbnail vanished, leaving Nancie and Will in amused silence.

"Tell me again," Nancie said, "why we ever thought scripts were enough?"

Will smiled. "Because we hadn't met the digital teammates who could write and rewrite them for us."

3.1 From Pins To Prompts: How Adam Smith's 250-Year-Old Theory Is Driving the Agentic AI Revolution

Adam Smith (1723-1790) was a Scottish economist and moral philosopher who was a pioneer in the field of political economics. Often dubbed the *father of economics*, Smith earned the epithet as a result of his seminal work, *An Inquiry into the Nature and Causes of the Wealth of Nations* (1776) (https://en.wikipedia.org/wiki/Adam_Smith?utm_source=chatgpt.com).

In it, he introduced the now-famous principle of the division of labor. Which argues that breaking production into specialized tasks lets each worker master a narrow slice of the process, multiplying overall output.

For example, if a shoe factory owner assigned one worker to creating the soles and one to making the laces, a factory can turn out far more pairs per hour than a single cobbler ever could. This is because of the time saved by simplifying and specializing each workers' responsibilities (i.e., many hands makes light work).

An ancillary benefit of this approach is the potential for innovation in tools and machinery. Specialists, immersed in a single step, are the first to spot how a new jig or machine could do it faster.

What's quite mind-blowing is that these insights that sparked the Industrial Revolution more than two centuries ago are becoming the cornerstone of yet another economic evolution. For years, human knowledge workers have been accepting more, diverse responsibilities to keep up with the chaotic demands of the digital economy. They look to "grow their portfolio" to appear as though they are doing more than their peers or competitors.

This pivot from what makes specialization so special has had almost ironic consequences. Lateral stretches of effort have slowly and silently made our knowledge workers, our leaders, and our subject matter experts less effective at each individual task they perform.

Nancie: "Will, with all that is going on with Agentic AI, I've been thinking about Industrial Revolution which brought me to Adam Smith's concepts of the division of labor. It's fascinating how a concept from the 1700s is suddenly relevant again with AI."

Will: "You mean the idea that breaking work into specialized tasks makes everything more efficient? It's wild how his pin factory metaphor feels like a blueprint for agentic AI."

Nancie: "Exactly. Smith showed that when each worker focused on just one part of the process, like drawing out the wire or attaching the head, they produced way more pins than one person doing everything. The parallel I see today is in how we're now using digital agents to break apart the 'knowledge work' we've been lumping together for decades."

Will: "Right. It's like we reversed Smith's insight for a while. Knowledge workers became generalists, juggling emails, meetings, project plans, reporting, because companies downsized and expected more with fewer people."

Nancie: "And ironically, that diluted their impact. When you're doing ten things, how deep can you really go on any one of them?"

Will: "Which brings us to agentic AI. Now, instead of expecting a person to manage everything, we can assign tasks to digital agents trained for specific responsibilities. Like having one agent manage your calendar, another draft your performance summaries, another analyze your pipeline."

Nancie: "Smith had his pin factory. We've got our digital workforce. And just like the Industrial Revolution accelerated output by specializing human labor, the Agentic AI Revolution scales knowledge work by doing the same, only now with autonomy."

Will: "The kicker? These agents don't burn out, don't context-switch inefficiently, and can continuously learn. That's not just scaling, it's compounding."

Nancie: "And it shifts how we think about productivity. It's not about how much more a human can carry, it's about how we distribute the load intelligently."

Will: "So, in a way, we've gone from pins to prompts, from crafting tools for labor to crafting digital collaborators that extend human capability."

Nancie: "And now the big question for leaders is: how do you organize your workforce, human and digital, for this next leap?"

Sound relatable?

Unfortunately, some of this behavior has been out of pure necessity. Most companies can't afford to hire one person for each responsibility and, particularly in the small and medium business landscape, there is an expectation that you "wear multiple hats".

This is why the topic of this book is the "Agentic AI Revolution" because this expectation is no longer true. You can provision an agent to book your lunch appointments, one to do your emails, and one to evaluate and write your performance review.

Smith showed that specialization scales humans; the next step is to ask how autonomy turns digital workers (i.e., agents) into colleagues.

3.2 What Makes Something Agentic?

A calendar alert blinks "Customer-Credit Risk Spike see triage." Will opens the dashboard, expecting the usual red-flag list, but nothing appears.

"System glitch?" he mutters.

A voice icon lights up.

Nova (Risk-Triage Agent): "Not a glitch I postponed the alert. Overnight inventory news invalidated yesterday's credit scores. Re-running my model now."

Nancie arches an eyebrow. "Since when does the agent reschedule its own jobs?"

Nova: "Since my last update. My goal is accurate risk ranking, not clock-chiming. When external data shifts beyond a 3% volatility threshold, I pause, retrain, and seek new human guidance if confidence drops."

Will whistles. "Old RPA would've dumped stale numbers into Finance just to meet SLA."

Nova continues.

"I'll need your sign-off on the revised threshold. Meanwhile, I've queued e-mails to customers who might see delayed approvals, the drafts are in your Outbox, tone set to 'conciliatory + options.'"

Nancie clicks one open. "It apologized, proposes revised terms, and cites the commodity spike. That's context in action."

Will leans back. "Autonomy, situational awareness, feedback loop: textbook agency."

Nova chimes again.

"Clarifying: textbook Level-2 agency. I still escalate strategic policy changes. Shall I log this as a learning instance for tomorrow's reflection run?"

"Do it," Will says. "And Nova nice catch."

CHAPTER 3   UNDERSTANDING AGENCY—WHAT MAKES AGENTIC AI A TEAMMATE, NOT A TOOL

Nova: "Thank you. Objective alignment reinforced."

The icon fades. Nancie smiles. "Hard to call that a tool. Tools don't negotiate their deadlines with you."

Will jots three bullets on the whiteboard:

1. *Goal-seeking autonomy*
2. *Real-time context sensing*
3. *Self-improvement via feedback*

"Welcome to the definition section," he says. "Let's show readers why those three traits turn code into a teammate."

The Three Pillars of Agency

Pillar 1: Goal-seeking autonomy

Have you ever worked with someone who just *makes things happen,* even if the final path looks nothing like the plan?

This is what is designed into the AI agents of today. They are driven by a clearly stated *outcome* ("minimize cash-flow risk," "book the cheapest on-time flight") and, at the same time, are free to choose the sequence of actions that best achieves it.

This is drastically different from a procedural script that must be told *every* click or API call. They can be given guard-rails, not micro-steps; they fill in the "how." You don't have to babysit them every step of the way. You can build that trust gradually, treat the agent like a new intern or recent grad, expanding its freedom only as it proves itself.

For example, you could have a travel agent where you provide the instruction: *"keep arrival before 9 a.m.; budget ≤ $700"* and it alternates between airlines, trains, and car services until the constraint is met.

The ability of LLMs to understand the meaning of natural language instructions and convert those instructions into paths for conducting a series of activities provides better performance with less setup. You don't need to spend time creating dialogue trees or brittle switch statements and yet you get exponentially better functionality.

For instance, take our travel agent scenario.

With a **traditional dialog tree,** you would hard-code every branch:

- "Press 1 for flights, 2 for trains…"
- If the fare tops $700, route to a scripted apology, reset, and start again.

- Add a new carrier? You update menus, audio files, and retest every path.

- Quarterly maintenance means hours of UAT just to keep the tree from breaking.

By contrast, a **natural-language agent** needs only one, expandable prompt: "Find me an itinerary that lands before 9 a.m. and costs under $700."

The model infers intent, juggles flights, trains, and ride-shares, and even discovers new carrier APIs the moment they appear—no menu edits, no branching logic. Ongoing upkeep shrinks to reviewing guard-rail logs and tweaking a threshold or two, while the agent continuously refines its own search strategy in the background.

Pillar 2: Context Awareness

What's never been possible with any technology, let alone automation tools, before the invention of the LLM is the ability to not just store commands but also the underlying meaning of what's stored. With the ability to store conversation and prompt history, AI agents have the awareness to continuously sense their operating environment, including data, policy, even a teammate's away-status, and adjust plans mid-flight.

Two recent Microsoft patterns sharpen that edge:

- **Model Context Protocol (MCP)** wraps each prompt in a lightweight "context envelope"—schemas, business rules, user roles—so the agent always knows *why* it's acting, not just *what* to call.

- **Agent-to-Agent (A2A) orchestration** lets specialists broadcast intent and status to one another, handing off work the way humans pass a baton across shifts.

So the agent isn't a blind batch job. If their instructions call for checking in on current information or they've learned from previous runs that they should check this kind of information at some point in the process to get better results, they'll call whatever MCP Server, API, or other data point they need to make the pivot.

For example, think back to our credit-risk AI agent from earlier. It can pause the approval process if a 3% swing in commodity prices changes margin exposure, retrain its model, and then resume.

Are you serious?! What workflow or pre-defined sequence could ever even come close to that level of adaptability!

Pillar 3: Self-Improvement Via Feedback

With context understanding comes the ability to read between the lines. Every execution is an experiment that feeds the next: AI agents can log outcomes, analyze deltas, and update their own policy (with or without a request for a human update), all without a redeploy.

This blows the "set-and-forget" model out of the water. No more worrying whether the model will be frozen shortly after the first release. CICD pipelines become fluid, MLOps doesn't have to version and retrain every time there's a slight trend of data drift.

AI agents are smart enough to recognize that the most important data you can possibly use is last run's feedback. They are not trying to memorize a pattern but develop a flexible policy that can fit all kinds of complexity curves.

Take Cal for example, it spots that last month's reconciliation paused for 17 manual overrides; clusters the override reasons and suggests a new rule to auto-handle 80% of them next month.

This may be the most important difference when thinking about how the technology functions. For so long, the whole field of Data Science was committed to finding ways to create and train a model that fit a particular problem; only to fail and then try to fit the problem around how they create and train the model. With AI agent's ability to self-improve, you can focus less on thinking ahead of what could break the model and spend more time focusing on managing and designing ways to grow the AI agent in ways it can't recognize for itself.

Of course, with great power comes great responsibility. While agentic AI is turbo-charging productivity, it also introduces a new class of risks (technical, ethical, and legal) that demand purposeful governance and, quite possibly, fresh counsel in the boardroom.

Next, we'll unpack what to be mindful of when deploying digital employees and how to keep innovation from outrunning oversight.

CHAPTER 3   UNDERSTANDING AGENCY—WHAT MAKES AGENTIC AI A TEAMMATE, NOT A TOOL

3.3 Degrees of Freedom: A Taxonomy

Would you really be surprised if we told you that not all AI agents have the same level of agency? Depending on the scenario, the data available, the preference of the users and many other things, there are an assortment of agentic characteristics that are worth taking note of.

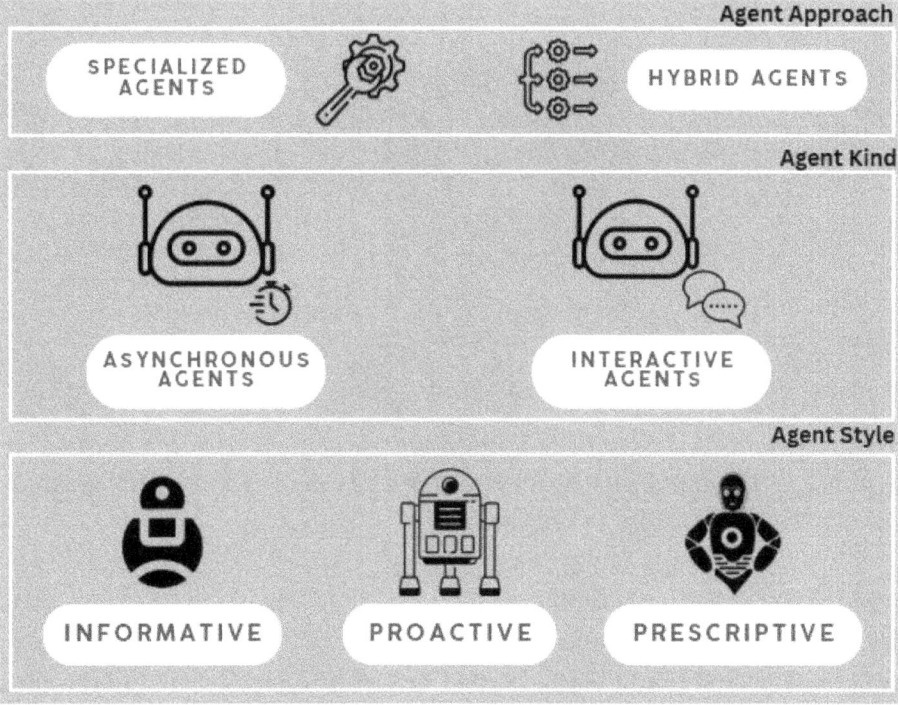

Figure 3-1. *Agent Taxonomy Overview: Three dimensions of design: Approach (Specialized vs. Hybrid), Kind (Asynchronous vs. Interactive), and Style (Informative, Proactive, Prescriptive). Combine them to tailor an agent to the job*

See Figure 3-1 for the three "dials" you'll turn when designing an agent: **Approach, Kind, and Style**. Treat it like a menu: pick one setting for each dial to ensure the agent capability aligns with the job, then adjust over time as trust and guard-rails mature.

CHAPTER 3   UNDERSTANDING AGENCY—WHAT MAKES AGENTIC AI A TEAMMATE, NOT A TOOL

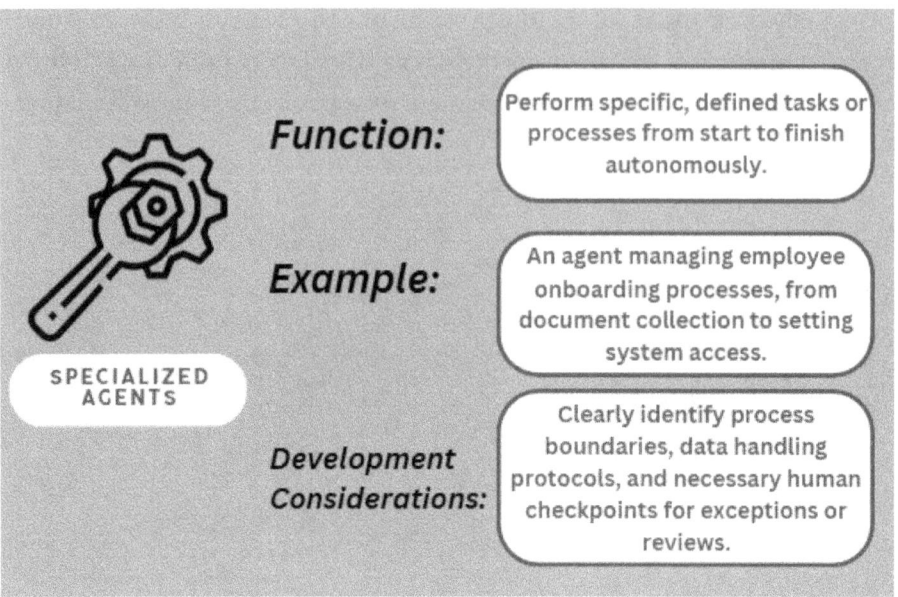

Figure 3-2. *Specialized Agents: Single-purpose agents that run a defined process end-to-end (e.g., onboarding). Success depends on crisp scope, clear data protocols, and human check-points for exceptions*

Figure 3-2 shows the best starting point for a single, repeatable workflow. In these cases, keep your scope crisp with a clear objective and a pass/fail acceptance test; a high degree of specialization is how we start to bring Smith's division of labor into code.

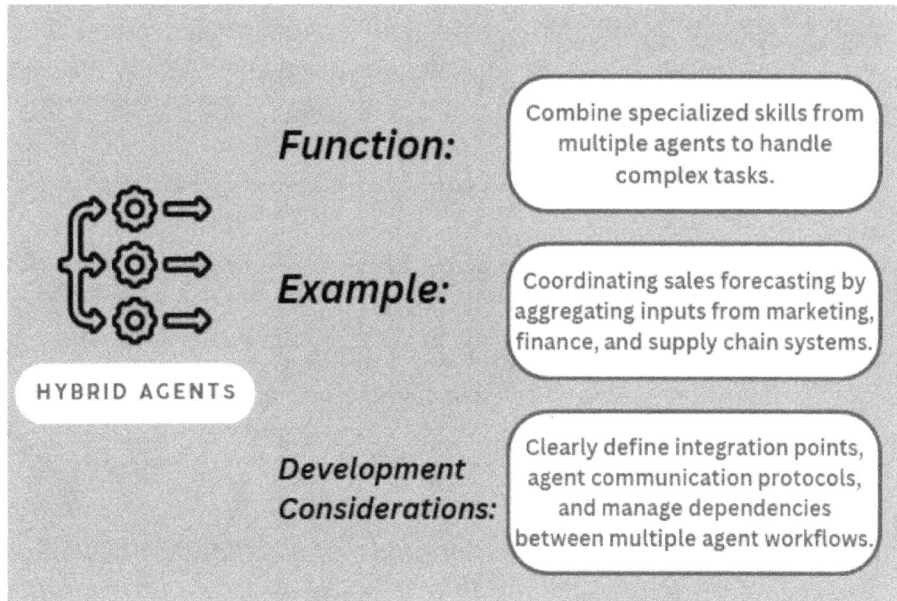

Figure 3-3. *Hybrid Agents: Orchestrators that coordinate multiple specialists across domains (e.g., forecasting from marketing, finance, and supply chain). Design requires explicit integration points and inter-agent communication rules*

When a process spans teams or systems, switch to a **Hybrid** orchestrator (Figure 3-3). It coordinates several specialists to complete one or many tasks. In these cases, you'll want to define handoffs and shared memory up front to avoid "agent chaos."

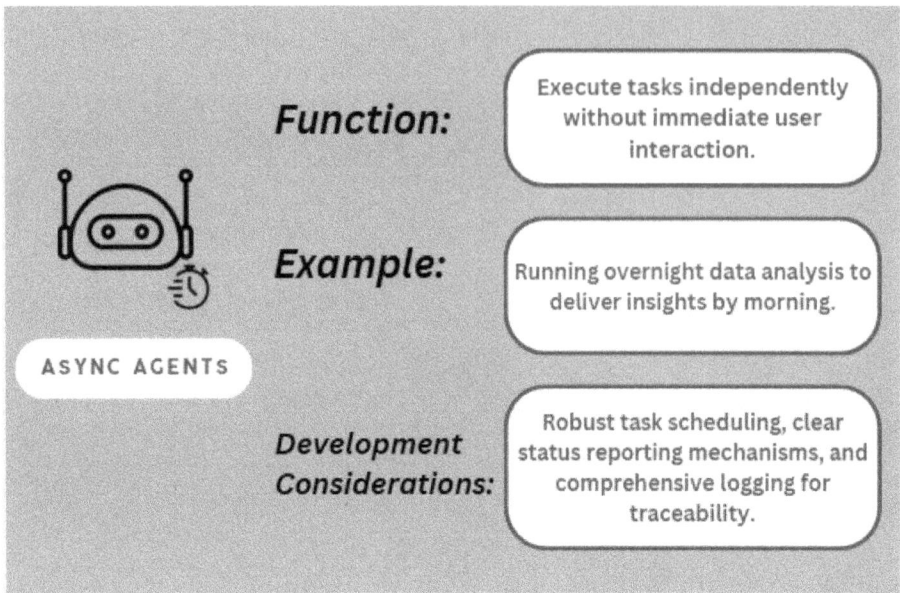

Figure 3-4. *Asynchronous Agents: Background workers that execute without a user present (e.g., overnight analytics). Prioritize scheduling, status reporting, and thorough logging for traceability*

Use **Asynchronous** agents for overnight or background work (Figure 3-4). Success lives in scheduling, idempotency, and logging. If it fails at 2 a.m., you want a clean audit log to troubleshoot with at 9 a.m.

CHAPTER 3   UNDERSTANDING AGENCY—WHAT MAKES AGENTIC AI A TEAMMATE, NOT A TOOL

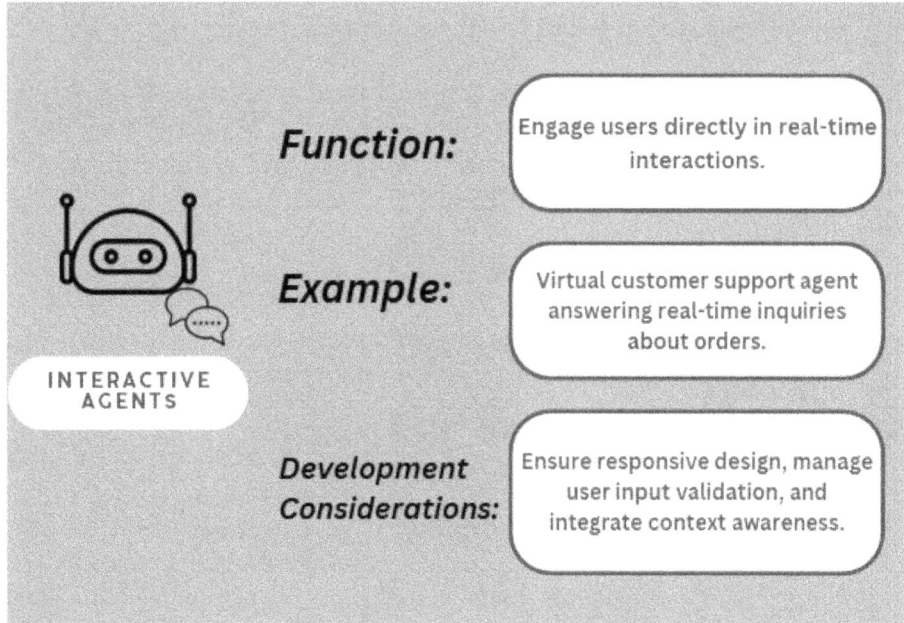

Figure 3-5. *Interactive Agents: Real-time conversational helpers (e.g., order-status support chatbot). Reliability hinges on responsive UX, input validation, and strong context awareness*

Figure 3-5 highlights **Interactive** agents for real-time help. These are usually your chatbots, Copilots, or live assistants. For these use cases, prioritize a responsive UX, input validation, and clear escalation so the conversation stays useful under the pressure of real-time requests.

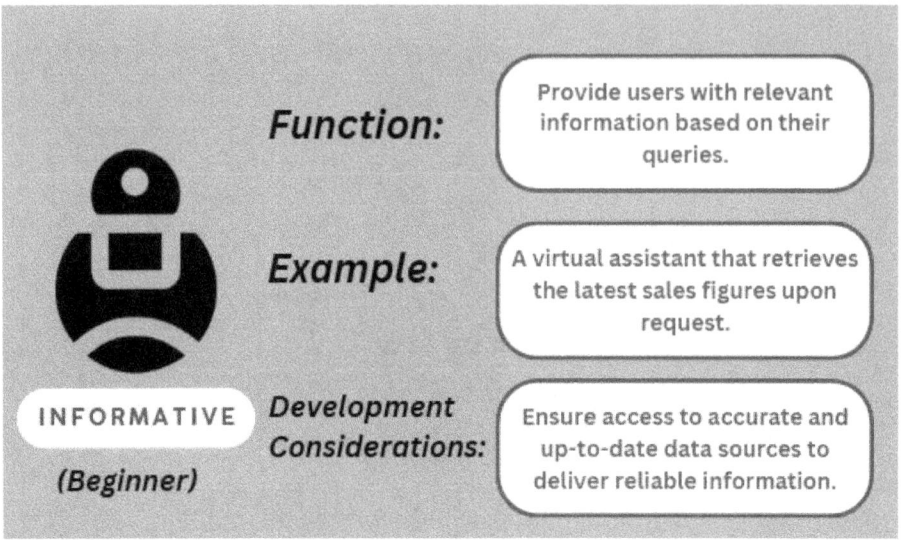

Figure 3-6. *Informative Style (Beginner): Agents that answer questions and surface facts or summaries (e.g., "latest sales figures"). Ensure access to accurate, current sources to keep answers trustworthy*

Start here. **Informative** agents (Figure 3-6) answer questions and summarize signals. They are great for quick wins while you harden data quality and governance.

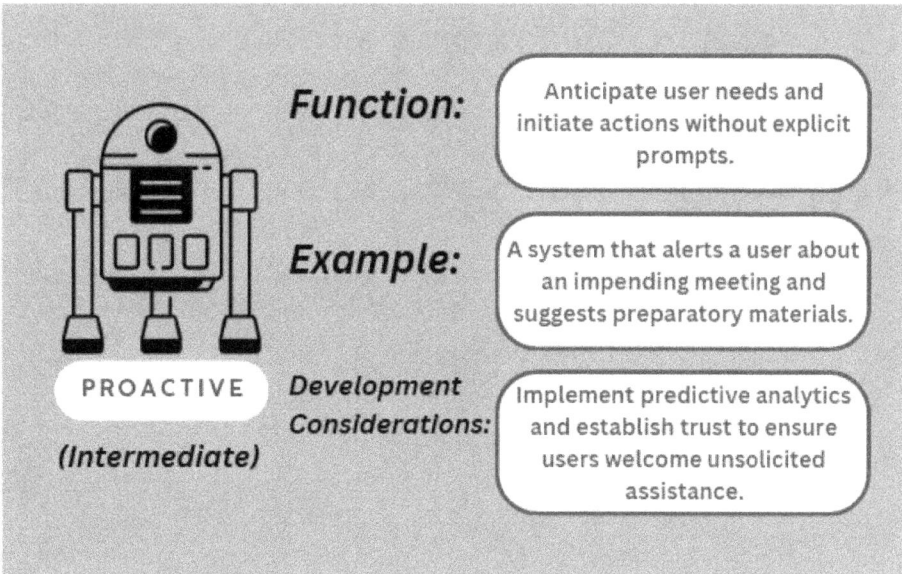

Figure 3-7. *Proactive Style (Intermediate): Agents that anticipate needs and nudge users (e.g., pre-meeting briefs, anomaly alerts). Implement prediction plus guard-rails so unsolicited help builds, not erodes, trust*

Proactive agents (Figure 3-7) nudge users before issues escalate. In these cases, you should use opt-in and pair metrics with counter-metrics (e.g., alert latency with alert fatigue) to keep trust high.

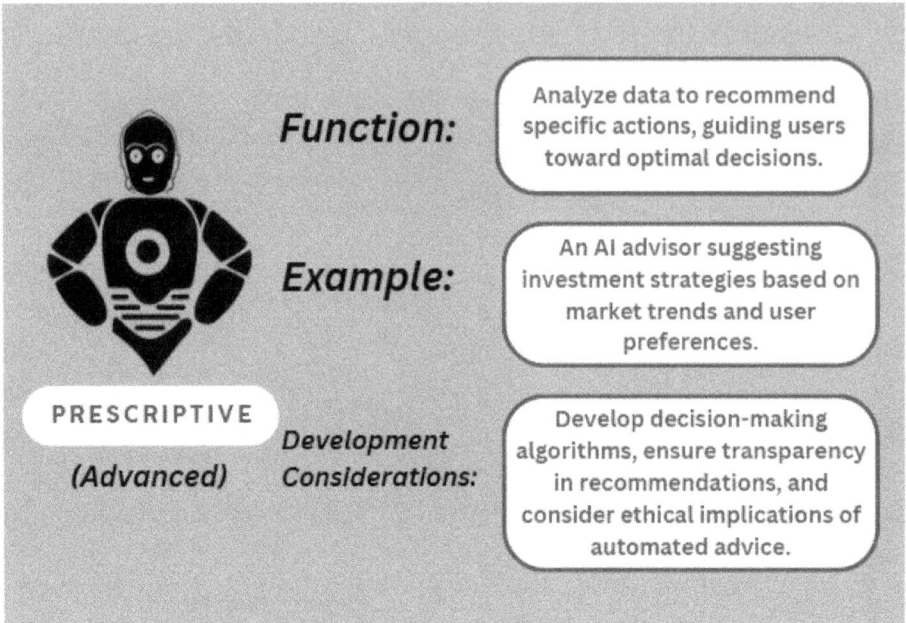

Figure 3-8. *Prescriptive Style (Advanced): Agents that recommend or trigger next best actions (e.g., investment rebalancing). Require transparent reasoning, robust decision policies, and ethical review*

When the system should recommend or trigger actions, you're in **Prescriptive** territory (Figure 3-8). Though this is the highest form of agent autonomy to date, it requires detailed rationale logging and HITL checkpoints for any high-risk activities; we'll expand on the governance aspects of this in Chapter 6.

CHAPTER 3   UNDERSTANDING AGENCY—WHAT MAKES AGENTIC AI A TEAMMATE, NOT A TOOL

Agent Type	When To Create
Specialized	You have a clearly scoped, end-to-end business process (e.g., order to cash, employee onboarding) that can run autonomously.
Hybrid	Your solution spans multiple domains (e.g., marketing, finance, supply chain) and you need to orchestrate several specialized agents/data sources together.
Asynchronous	Tasks can execute offline or in batch (e.g., nightly data processing, batch report generation) without blocking users.
Interactive	You need a conversational interface or real-time guidance (e.g., virtual support chat, guided form-filling).
Informative	The primary goal is to surface timely insights or summaries (e.g., daily dashboards, KPI alerts) to support decisions.
Proactive	You want the system to anticipate needs and trigger actions/notifications (e.g., low-inventory alerts, anomaly warnings).
Prescriptive	Users require concrete recommendations or next-best actions based on data analysis (e.g., investment rebalancing advice).

Figure 3-9. *When to Create Which Agent: Quick reference that maps each agent type to its ideal use case; use it to pick the right Approach, Kind, and Style combination for your scenario*

Figure 3-9 is your quick decision matrix; you can use this to match your scenarios to the different agent types during your workshops. Use it to pick a starting combo (often Specialized × Async × Informative), then evolve toward Proactive/Prescriptive extensions or capabilities as confidence grows.

Thank you for powering through that bit of pedagogy☺. And your reward is…scenarios!

Scenario A—*The HR Help Hub*

Problem. A 600-person scale-up drowns in onboarding tickets: laptop orders, payroll forms, system-access requests.

Characteristic	Choice	Why it fits
Approach	Hybrid	Needs to orchestrate IT, Finance, Facilities micro-agents.
Kind	Interactive	New hires fire off questions in real time.
Style	Proactive	Reminds managers to upload org-chart, nudges finance when banking info is missing.

Why not prescriptive? Recommending "which role to hire next" crosses into HR strategy, outside this AI agent's charter. Keep scope crisp.

Scenario B—Overnight Ledger Reconciler

Problem. Finance must match cash entries to invoices before the 8 a.m. board packet.

Characteristic	Choice	Why it fits
Approach	Specialized	One end-to-end process, repeatable nightly.
Kind	Asynchronous	Batch window 01:00–05:00, no human in loop unless anomaly.
Style	Proactive	Flags variance >2%, suggests GL corrections.

Scenario C—Sales-Forecast Orchestrator

Problem. Quarter-end numbers swing wildly because Marketing, Finance, and Supply-Chain data land in silos.

Characteristic	Choice	Why it fits
Approach	Hybrid	Pulls from three domains, writes one forecast.
Kind	Asynchronous + Interactive	Batch ingest overnight **and** chat command *"/forecast update"* during the day.
Style	Informative → Proactive (evolves)	Starts as dashboard generator; graduates to nudging reps when pipeline gaps appear.

What's most important to remember is that the best AI agents are designed with combinations of these approaches, styles, and kinds, and you may find more that help you distinguish the ways to build the AI agents that work in your world. Use these references as a starter pack of sorts to start building your very own fleet of autonomous teammates.

Now that you have a clear way of designing your agents, let's dive into methods you can use to divide up their work accordingly.

3.4 Digital Division-of-Labor Playbook

The genius of Adam Smith's division of labor wasn't an endless conveyor belt of mind-numbing tasks. It was the idea of empowering each contributor with deep, specialized knowledge and chaining those touchpoints together into a graceful, scalable system.

We can replicate that today in our agentic world only at cloud speed and global scale by simply (and ironically) picking a process and following a sequence of five steps:

Step 1: Map the Value Chain

This should be one of the easiest parts. You are either the subject matter expert (SME) or know someone who is. The idea is to tap into the well of business domain knowledge within your company to piece together every handoff, every context switch, every known complexity, and anything else you can use to put together the clearest, most holistic understanding of how the process operates today.

This helps uncover the three most critical things:

1. How much domain understanding about a process is documented and how much is in your team's head.
2. Where the real bottlenecks are and what issues they cause.
3. The hidden decision points that will make perfect micro goals.

You can use something like a sticky note swim lane or a Miro board (online brainstorming tool) to document this.

Step 2: Carve Out Your Micro Goals

This may seem straightforward, but there is an art to sizing these agentic solution functionalities. You want to keep them small enough to master but large enough to matter.

Think of a micro-goal as the smallest slice of work that

1. Starts when it's obvious the input is ready to be worked on
2. Produces a clearly testable output
3. Can be judged *in isolation*—without rereading the entire process log

Essentially, you should keep breaking a handoff into smaller steps until even someone new to the project can tell, from just the step's local artifacts, whether it succeeded.

For example, let's say the handoff is called "Ship the customer's order." This is too big; a human would have to scroll through order notes, payment status, stock levels, carrier rules, etc., to verify success.

Here's what the handoff looks like broken down into micro-goals:

ID	Micro-goal	"Done" evidence a junior analyst can see instantly
G-1	Generate pick list and reserve inventory	PDF pick list stored + inventory rows flagged "reserved"
G-2	Create shipping label and book carrier	Label file saved + carrier API returns tracking #
G-3	Update ERP order line with tracking #	Order record shows TrackingStatus = "Booked"

Now any newcomer can open a single document or database row per goal and answer "yes, that part's finished" without hunting through previous steps.

What makes this so important for building agents is that it makes validation a simple acceptance test. The file exists, the field updated, confidence ≥ 0.9, the clearer the metric of success, the more successful the AI agent will be.

It also accelerates troubleshooting. You can inspect the logs on each failing micro-goal rather than trying to find the needle in the stack of all process logs.

Finally, each micro-goal maps neatly to one agent persona which is step 3.

Step 3: Match Each Goal to an Agent Persona

Now that you know what kind of characteristics and attributes are available for each AI agent, pick an Approach—Kind—Style combo (from § 3.3) for every micro-goal. This ensures the agent's "job description" fits the work, just like hiring the right specialist.

A quick artifact you could create to capture this would be a table that maps each micro goal to the Agent Persona combination you think is most appropriate for its role in the process. Here's a snippet of that you could plug into a Microsoft Copilot Studio agent:

Field	Entry
Agent Name	CreditCheckPro
Micro-Goal ID	G-2 · Credit Check
Approach × Kind × Style	Specialized × Asynchronous × Proactive
Objective	"Assess each new order's credit risk and either approve automatically or escalate."
Success Criteria	• *Approval decision returned ≤ 2 min* • *False-approval rate < 0.5%*
Guard-Rails/Constraints	• *Confidence ≥ 0.90* • *Do not access PII beyond credit-score API* • *API spend ≤ $0.05 per order*
Data and Tools	ERP order feed, external credit-score API, foreign exchange (FX) rate service
Escalation Path	Flag to Finance-OnCall Teams channel with JSON payload
Self-Improvement Loop	After each run, log decision and outcome to */agent_logs/creditcheck*. Retrain weekly on misclassified cases after human review.
Examples of Autonomy	• Auto-approve orders ≤ $25 k when confidence ≥ 0.95. • Pause the flow and request FX refresh if EUR/USD shifts > 1%.

Step 4: Define Shared Memory and Baton Passes

Some agents in your workstream are going to need to work together. Some will be completely isolated. Perhaps because of the data they interact with or based on department communications within your organization.

CHAPTER 3   UNDERSTANDING AGENCY—WHAT MAKES AGENTIC AI A TEAMMATE, NOT A TOOL

The focus of this step is to decide what data lives where. What data stays in the AI agents' memory? What do they all have access to? What lives in a particular knowledge base? Does feedback get shared to every AI agent or only the one it is addressed to? This prevents data clashes and orphan processes as the fleet grows.

This could look like a lightweight JSON schema with an event trigger list. For example:

```json
{
  "schema_version": "1.0",
  "agent_name": "CreditCheckPro",
  "memory_layers": {
    "working_memory": {
      "order_id": "string",
      "customer_id": "string",
      "risk_score": "float",
      "confidence": "float",
      "timestamp": "ISO-8601"
    },
    "knowledge_base": {
      "customer_master": "s3://o2c-kb/customer_master.parquet",
      "policy_thresholds": "s3://o2c-kb/credit_policy.yml"
    },
    "reflections_log": "s3://o2c-logs/creditcheck/{date}/"
  },
  "guard_rails": {
    "confidence_threshold": 0.90,
    "max_api_cost_usd": 0.05,
    "pii_scope": ["customer_id", "risk_score"]
  },
  "handoff_config": {
    "payload_uri": "s3://o2c-handoff/{order_id}.json",
    "events": [
      {
        "event": "creditApproved",
        "target_agent": "FulfilShipBot"
      },
      {
        "event": "creditEscalated",
        "target_team": "Finance_OnCall"
      }
    ]
  }
}
```

Step 5: Bolt on Guardrails Up Front

Autonomy without governance is a liability, not a feature. AI agents are guardrail hungry! As we discussed earlier, their level of freedom gives them the ability to take unorthodox roads to their solutions, so you have clearly defined for them what's appropriate and what's not. Create confidence gates, cost ceilings, time-boxes, and compliance checks so the AI agent can leverage the strength of its adaptability without causing you unnecessary headaches.

If you're looking for a simple rule of thumb to get started in this process, it's best to start with a minimal agent (Specialized × Async × Informative). Have it connected to one data source and perform a task with the data from it on a scheduled interval.

"One of my first agent projects was with a client who just wanted to send out automated field operation summaries every morning. All we did was take the key data points from their field database, run an LLM over them to create that summary and then had the workflow automatically send the created summary by email. Simple, powerful and very easy to control," Will said.

"Perfect way to start with Agentic AI," Nancie replied. *"Simple, easy to see the value, and very tight guardrails to keep the value focused."*

Let's go through a mini case study to help bring this all to life.

Order-to-Cash in Four Digital Specialists

Imagine you run a mid-market manufacturing firm shipping hundreds of orders each night. You decide to replace a brittle RPA spaghetti-flow with four purpose-built agents, each owning one micro-goal of the order-to-cash chain. Here's how the playbook materializes in practice:

Station	Agent Persona (Approach × Kind × Style)	Hard Guard-rail
1 · Order Intake	Interactive × Specialized × Informative	*Escalate unknown SKU*
2 · Credit Check	Async × Specialized × Proactive	*Confidence ≥ 0.90*
3 · Fulfill and Ship	Hybrid × Async × Proactive	*API spend ≤ $15 per run*
4 · Invoice and Collect	Interactive × Specialized × Prescriptive	*Variance ≤ $500*

How the quartet plays out overnight:

1. Order Intake Agent—"GreeterBot"

   12:05 a.m. A new EDI order lands. GreeterBot parses the payload, validates each SKU against the product master, and posts a confirmation in Teams. When it spots an unfamiliar SKU, the *Escalate unknown SKU* guard-rail kicks in: it pauses processing and pings the product manager for mapping. Nothing downstream runs on bad data.

2. Credit Check Agent—"RiskRanger"

   As soon as GreeterBot labels the order *Clean*, RiskRanger wakes up. Operating asynchronously, it scores the customer using last-minute FX rates and receivables history. If its probability of default dips below 0.90 confidence, it autopasses; otherwise, it creates a high-priority task for Finance. The proactive style means it also nudges Sales with, "FYI—customer near limit; consider deposit on next order."

3. Fulfill and Ship Agent—"RouteRunner"

   At 01:40 a.m. RouteRunner orchestrates two micro-services: warehouse pick-list generation and multi-carrier price shopping. Because shipping APIs bill per request, its guard-rail watches real-time spend. If quotes start to exceed $15 per order, RouteRunner falls back to cached carrier rates and logs the event for review—avoiding silent cost creep while still shipping on time.

4. Invoice and Collect Agent—"LedgerLiaison"

   Once tracking numbers hit the ERP, LedgerLiaison drafts the invoice, applies any rebate programs, and emails the customer. The *Prescriptive* style allows it to recommend "Pay-Now" ACH links when average days-sales-outstanding exceeds 45. But it must respect the $500 variance ceiling: if the calculated invoice differs from the order's net price by more than $500, it pauses and routes the case to Accounts Receivable.

Why the design works:

- **Clear micro-goals**: No agent sees the whole world; each master's its slice.

- **Persona fit**: Interactive for front-of-house clarifications, async for heavy lifting, prescriptive only where policy allows.

- **Guard-rails first**: Cost, confidence, and compliance are coded day one, so autonomy never outruns oversight.

- **Shared memory**: All four write JSON snapshots to a single */order-state* container, enabling seamless baton passes and painless audits.

3.5 Bringing the Pieces Together

Adam Smith's pin factory taught us that specialization multiplies output; by reframing that lesson for the digital age, we saw how Cal, Nova, and a troop of purpose-built AI agents can shoulder specialized, well-defined goals (budget recaps, credit triage, ledger clean-ups) while humans kept their heads free for judgment. From there we dug into the three pillars of agency (goal-seeking autonomy, context awareness, self-improvement) and saw how even a single prompt can replace pages of brittle dialog trees.

A quick taxonomy then showed that agency isn't one-size-fits-all: Approach × Kind × Style lets you dial the right degree of freedom for HR chatbots, overnight reconciliations, sales-forecast orchestrators, and beyond. Finally, the Digital Division-of-Labor Playbook walked you through mapping a value chain, carving micro-goals, matching personas, wiring shared memory, and bolting on guard-rails, culminating in an order-to-cash case where four agents shaved hours off-cycle time without sacrificing control.

These explorations have shown what makes software agentic and how to design it so code behaves like a trusted teammate, not just a faster macro.

Leadership Checklist: Designing Your First Agent Fleet

☑ **Start with a Pin Map:** White-board every handoff; look for hidden decision points and tribal knowledge.

☑ **Define Micro-Goals:** Write "done" tests any newcomer can verify in one click or query.

- ☑ **Pick Personas, Not Just Prompts:** For each micro-goal, choose an Approach–Kind–Style that matches risk, tempo, and user expectations.

- ☑ **Specify Guard-Rails Day 1:** Confidence gates, cost ceilings, time-boxes, and PII scope should live beside the prompt, not in a later ticket.

- ☑ **Plan Shared Memory:** Agree which data stays local, which belongs in a common knowledge base, and how agents hand off payloads.

- ☑ **Stage Autonomy:** Begin with Specialized × Async × Informative; graduate to proactive or prescriptive only after metrics prove reliability.

- ☑ **Log Reflections:** Store one JSON line per run so agents—and auditors—can learn from every outcome.

- ☑ **Pair Metrics with Counter-Metrics:** Balance speed with quality (e.g., approval latency *and* false-positive rate).

- ☑ **Shadow and Upskill Humans:** Rotate staff through "agent-ops" shifts so domain expertise grows alongside automation.

- ☑ **Road-Test in a Sandbox:** Simulate volatile inputs (price spikes, bad SKUs) before unleashing autonomy on live customers.

Will flips the last slide of their workshop. "Pins, prompts, personas, playbooks, that's a lot of theory."

Nancie nods toward the metrics dashboard Cal just pushed. "Theory that's begging for proof. Let's show what happens when these agents hit real KPIs."

Cal's icon pulses. "Preliminary data indicates a 37% reduction in reconciliation cycle-time over the pilot period. Shall I compile a comparative report?"

"Exactly what Chapter 4 needs," *Will says, grinning.* "Next stop: the numbers."

Nancie closes her laptop. "We've drawn the blueprints, now we test the steel."

CHAPTER 4

Why Agentic Capabilities Outperform Traditional AI

The sun spills gold across the asphalt as I steer my service truck into the silent serenity of the company lot at first light. My name is Mike, and I've been a field technician for the past five years. I'm familiar with every frayed cable, flickering screen, and faulty fuse this job can throw at me.

I've seen it all: the long hours, the frustration of hunting down hard-to-find solutions to complex problems, the constant juggling of paper forms and outdated systems to log service tickets. It's a routine that has become all too familiar. Every day, I rely on my tablet, flipping through notes from previous visits, reading service manuals, and double-checking troubleshooting guides, all while trying to stay on schedule. And while the process is necessary, it often feels like there's got to be a better way to work smarter, not harder.

Today, I'm headed to a customer's home who's been experiencing intermittent service disruptions. It's a repeat issue that's been lingering for weeks, and no one seems to be able to figure out why the signal keeps dropping. I've been here before, trying to track down the root cause, but so far, all I've done is patch things up temporarily.

Pulling up the driveway, I unlatch the toolbox in the truck bed, the metal catching the morning's misty chill, when my phone buzzes with an unfamiliar tone. It's a message from **our** *new* **AI-driven system**. *A couple of weeks ago, the company implemented a new tool called* **Copilot**, *a system designed to streamline field service operations. At first, I wasn't convinced. Another tool? Another system to learn? But the message I received today caught my attention: "***Copilot*** has detected a possible network issue in your area. It may be related to the customer's equipment, and a signal boost is recommended."*

I open up the **Copilot** *interface on my tablet and notice that it's already pulled up the customer's service history, including past issues and any diagnostic data gathered during previous visits. As I review the information, the system suggests a series of steps I could*

CHAPTER 4   WHY AGENTIC CAPABILITIES OUTPERFORM TRADITIONAL AI

follow, including updating the equipment firmware and testing the signal strength before even checking the equipment in person (would've been nice to know that before I drove all this way).

I pause. Could a few taps on this tablet truly trump five years of trial-and-error? Yet there it is, an elegant, evidence-based explanation I hadn't even considered. Suddenly, the monotony of my routine feels like an outdated issue, what part of my job can I reinvent next?

It's no secret that the AI world has been evolving at lightning speed but perhaps this lightning trajectory is simply a reflection of the business landscape we operate in today. Traditional AI tools have made significant strides in automating simple tasks like forecasting your Monthly Recurring Revenue (MRR), streamlining workflows like case triaging, and providing "little wins" for businesses but, as customer expectations shift, traditional AI, while still valuable, has begun to show its limitations. The static, one-trick pony systems of yesterday like chatbots and product recommendation systems simply aren't enough to meet the complex, dynamic demands of today's business landscape.

To this point, we've discussed what's inspired agentic AI, what gaps it appears to fill and what qualifies a system as "agentic." Now, we're shifting focus to what exactly allows agentic AI to outperform traditional AI in the real world.

Throughout this chapter, we'll show how agentic AI doesn't just deliver proactive recommendations; it breathes your business, its data, workflows, and objectives so intimately that it knows how to guide the team to the next best move for the business. We'll see how businesses can leverage **agentic AI** to achieve smarter decision-making, enhance customer interactions, and drive productivity at scale by reimagining how the central nervous system of their business thinks and operates (keyword think).

To demonstrate these capabilities, we'll explore real-world examples through our fictional company, TeleComX. This composite organization embodies our collective experience with real-world clients who have started leveraging agentic AI across sales, field service, and customer support. By integrating **Copilot** and **Azure AI**, companies like **TeleComX** can proactively detect and diagnose issues, conduct context-aware workflows on behalf of technicians, and resolve customer problems faster and more accurately.

As we journey through this chapter, you'll discover why **agentic AI** is the definition of truly intelligent systems, why it's essential for organizations to move beyond basic automation and AI systems, and how to capitalize on the next wave of AI innovation to create a more efficient, responsive, and scalable business.

4.1 Benchmark 1: Task Robustness

The difference between specialized and singular

Traditional AI systems, such as chatbots and ML-based automation, typically operate in a predefined and limited set of conditions. These systems are designed with the intention to perform specific, often single-output tasks (e.g., object detection in an image analysis) that naturally lack the ability to address complex, multistep issues or engage in meaningful interactions with users. They rely on knowing the answer ahead of time, making them less effective in scenarios that require managing a high degree of uncertainty.

As we discussed in Chapter 3, agentic AI is designed to tackle specific, loosely related tasks within defined goals and can adjust its behavior in real time to meet the needs of the user. Unlike traditional chatbots that follow a script, agentic AI can handle complex workflows that involve several actions, decision-making, and the ability to adapt to different scenarios.

Nancie:

"Will, the key difference here seems to be that traditional AI systems and automation are reactive, right? They respond based on what's explicitly programmed into them. They can't adjust or evolve in real-time the way agentic AI does."

Will:

"Precisely, Nancie. As an example, traditional chatbots are great for scripted responses to predictable queries. But when it comes to more complex situations, like troubleshooting a service issue or adjusting a bill based on new information, they fall short. Agentic AI, on the other hand, is built to understand situational dynamics and adapt. It can handle more nuanced scenarios, learn from each interaction, and provide a much more personalized and intuitive experience."

Context Awareness = Adaptability

One of the defining features of agentic AI is context awareness. Unlike traditional systems that provide generic responses, agentic AI is highly agile to the business function and specific interaction context. It can determine current intent as well as synthesize historical data points and real-time input, allowing it to tailor its responses or actions to the full picture, not just the one it's been programmed with.

For instance, Copilot integrated into Office 365 can understand what you need help with next (e.g., drafting an email or building a report) because of its connection to your data (past emails, PowerPoints, etc.) and the relationships between your data points (PowerPoints attached to specific email threads). This makes agentic AI far more powerful than traditional systems that can't take in new or changing information on the fly.

What makes this technological approach fundamentally different is that traditional chatbots are designed for known situations and requests based on a limited set of inputs. This often leads to static, repetitive, and non-useful interactions. The chatbot may handle simple requests, but if the customer's query goes beyond its knowledge base, the interaction is either escalated to a human agent or the conversation ends abruptly or goes into an endless circle, ultimately creating extreme frustration for the customer.

Copilot can engage in continuous, multidimensional (replies, creating artifacts for the user, completing tasks on their behalf) interactions with users and guide them to the right outcome. Agentic AI uses everything at its disposal to achieve the goals of the user in a personalized and efficient manner.

Will:

"I've seen a lot of businesses still using traditional chatbots, but with the evolution of Copilot and its integration into the Microsoft ecosystem, how do you see businesses transitioning to this more dynamic AI?"

Nancie: "Many clients worry it's a brand-new tool, but not in all cases. Copilot Studio, for example, actually builds on Power Virtual Agents. I showed a hesitant client that the underlying PVA technology they already trust now powers a more powerful, context-aware layer."

Will: "So it's not necessarily a giant leap, but it can be a natural next step?"

Nancie: "Exactly. Instead of static scripts, Copilot Studio AI Agents adapt in real time, engaging in deeper, multiturn dialogues, completing tasks inside apps, and learning from each interaction. By leveraging their existing PVA and Power Platform investments, clients can adopt Copilot with confidence."

Will: "That's the key: evolving from simple chatbots to AI that anticipates needs and guides users to outcomes without starting from scratch."

What's most important to understand here is that, by having the ability to dynamically process and act on information in real time, agentic AI, whether in Copilot or on its own, naturally operates at a higher level of robustness than a chatbot ever could. And this doesn't mean deleting your existing AI and automation infrastructure, it means you can upgrade it to capabilities that produce better customer and employee interactions and thereby fast-track you to improved business outcomes.

4.2 Benchmark 2: Self-Directed Problem Solving

Goal-Based Architectures

Traditional AI systems are designed to follow **fixed rules** or predefined scripts. When a user interacts with the system, it's only looking for pre-defined data points like specific keywords or phrases, and provides an output based on those predefined inputs. If the problem doesn't fit into the pre-programmed logic, it may not be addressed effectively, or it could require human intervention.

Agentic AI, on the other hand, is built with a **goal-based architecture**. It isn't just about responding to an inquiry, it's about solving a problem or achieving an outcome. For instance, if the goal is to resolve a service outage, it pulls live telemetry from network nodes, correlates that with historical service logs, and ranks the most likely root causes. Next, it sequences corrective actions: for example, it might push a targeted firmware patch to the customer's edge device, trigger a remote reboot, then run a post-fix signal test. At each step it evaluates success metrics (e.g., packet loss, latency), dynamically rerouting its plan if an initial fix doesn't fully clear the fault. Finally, it logs every action, updates the ticketing system with a summarized report, and pushes a personalized status update to the customer. Closing the loop with just the right amount of human prompting.

By contrast, a traditional AI system would struggle to string together those autonomous moves. A rules-based bot might recognize "outage" in a support ticket and reply with a generic checklist, "check your cables, reboot your modem," but it cannot assemble live diagnostics, apply a firmware update, verify results, and communicate back in one continuous flow. Most deviations from its script (for instance, a novel hardware revision or unusual signal anomaly) could trigger a dead end or immediate handoff to a human agent. In other words, a static decision tree can hint at what to try, but only a goal-based, self-directing agent can actually execute and adapt the fix in real time.

Multiturn Logic and State Retention

Traditional AI systems typically struggle with **multiturn interactions**, where the system loses track of the conversation's state between each exchange. Customers are often asked to repeat information multiple times, which leads to frustration and inefficiency.

In contrast, **agentic AI** utilizes **state retention**, allowing it to remember the context of ongoing interactions. It can hold and reference prior conversation points across multiple turns. This makes it capable of solving **multistep problems** and handling more dynamic conversations.

Imagine a customer calling about intermittent Wi-Fi drops across three rooms. In the first turn, the AI asks, "Which device are you using, the station in the living room, the bedroom extender, or the hallway repeater?" After the customer replies "bedroom extender," the agent pulls the device's serial number from the CRM and checks its firmware version. In turn two, it observes a mismatch and prompts, "Would you like me to push the latest patch now?" Once approved, it initiates the update and, in turn three, runs a live signal-strength test, then reports back, "Firmware updated and signal restored to 95% strength." Throughout this exchange, the agent retains the chosen device, the firmware state, even the customer's preference to proceed automatically next time, enabling a seamless, three-step fix in a single session.

A rules-based chatbot, by contrast, treats each message in isolation. It might start with, "Which device…?" but once the customer answers, it forgets that detail and asks again, or asks a different clarifying question that makes no sense. Any follow-up ("Did you want to update now?") comes with no awareness of which firmware version is installed or which device was named previously. If the customer says "yes," the bot can't execute the update; at best, it replies with a static link to instructions. At each turn, the lack of retained information forces repetition or dead-ends, turning a simple three-step resolution into a frustrating loop of questions and manual hand-offs. Only an agentic system with hardened state retention can carry the conversation thread, and the customer's request, end-to-end.

4.3 Benchmark 3: Automating Iteration

How Agents Handle Uncertainty and Environmental Change By Learning Through Execution

Unlike traditional systems, which often follow fixed rules and cannot improve autonomously, **agentic AI** systems **learn through execution**. They improve with each interaction, adapting to new situations and continuously refining their behavior. This self-learning capability makes **agentic AI** much more powerful over time as it evolves and becomes better at solving complex problems.

Consider a logistics hub where packages occasionally get misrouted. An agentic AI monitors conveyor sensors and delivery logs in real time. When it spots a spike in misroutes, it traces the fault to a misaligned scanner at Bay 7, then autonomously adjusts the scanner's recognition thresholds and reroutes affected parcels. Immediately after, it analyzes the post-adjustment error rate: seeing misroutes drop from 4% to 0.5%, it records the calibration parameters and flags that combination of ambient light and scanner settings to its memory. The next time a similar pattern appears, say, a new scanner model under a different warehouse light, it recalls the prior fix, applies a variant calibration, and achieves the same error reduction without human input. With every execution, the agent refines its own detection and remediation strategy, growing smarter through experience.

A conventional system might use a static machine-learning model trained on historical routing data. It can classify a misroute and even alert operators, but it cannot tweak scanner settings or measure results on the fly. Any model drift or novel scanner behavior goes unaddressed until a data scientist manually spot-checks the logs, retrains the model in a separate environment, and redeploys it, often days or weeks later. There's no closed-loop learning in production. Traditional AI follows the rules it was given; only an agentic system truly "learns by doing," continuously updating its playbook as it executes.

Nancie:

"Will, you know what's really powerful here? The way agentic AI can turn resolutions into valuable content for the knowledgebase. Instead of having someone manually create a guide for a recurring problem, the AI can automatically suggest, update, or even create new knowledge articles based on the solutions it provides."

Will:

" And the beauty is that it doesn't stop at creating new content, it also ensures that outdated information is updated. For example, if a solution that worked six months ago is no longer effective, the AI can revise existing articles, removing or updating outdated steps. It's a continuous improvement loop."

Nancie:

"Instead of employees spending time searching through old knowledgebase articles, the AI is doing the heavy lifting, ensuring that all technicians have access to relevant, up-to-date information, instantly."

Will:

"Right, and this is one of the key ways agentic AI helps drive operational efficiency. By automating knowledgebase management, businesses are not only improving their response times but also ensuring that best practices and successful solutions are automatically incorporated into day-to-day operations."

4.4 Agent Swarms: Coordinated Autonomy at Scale

Of course, the point of agents isn't to build one monolithic agent that does everything all the time. As explored in chapter 3, what gives agents their capabilities is the ability to be hyper-focused on specific business operations and their ability to communicate with other hyper-focused agents to complete chains of activities or processes.

What this concept looks like at scale can be observed from two distinct storylines:

- **Swarm intelligence** is first and foremost a technology story: it describes how simple, autonomous agents, each following a few local rules, interact until a higher-order intelligence emerges. Think of a flock of starlings or an ant colony: no single bird or ant sees the whole picture, yet together they solve problems far beyond any individual's reach.

- **Microsoft's "Journey to the Frontier Firm,"** by contrast, is an organizational-change narrative. It charts how leadership, culture, and ways of working must evolve as AI moves from personal assistants to these company-wide operation fleets.

We do this to showcase why leaders must keep the enterprise and the engineering disciplines in lock-step. Avoiding the classic trap where innovation outruns adoption (or vice-versa).

Level 1: Single-Agent Task Execution
Frontier-Firm Phase 1: Human with Assistant

At basecamp, a lone Copilot tackles one user's well-bounded task. Proof-reading a contract, triaging a help-desk ticket, summarizing a meeting. The breakthrough here is speed and accuracy for the individual; the broader organization feels only a ripple.

From the swarm-intelligence perspective, this is a single drone finding food close to the nest; useful, but not yet transformative. From the organizational perspective, Phase 1 is about familiarity and trust: every employee discovers that delegating micro-tasks to an AI sidekick frees them for higher-value work.

Level 2: Multi-Agent Coordination
Frontier-Firm Phase 2: Human–Agent Teams

Climbing higher, specialized agents begin to share a data fabric and hand work off to one another: one scans inbound leads, another enriches them with market intel, a third drafts personalized follow-ups. Humans remain the project managers, but coordination increasingly happens in the background.

Technologically, we now glimpse true swarm behavior; simple local rules ("when lead status = new, enrich then route") creating a composite workflow that no single agent could deliver alone. Organizationally, Phase 2 is the moment culture shifts from *using a helper tool* to *collaborating with digital colleagues*. Job descriptions stretch, KPIs adjust, and managers learn to orchestrate a mixed team of people and code.

Level 3: Enterprise-Wide Swarm Intelligence
Frontier-Firm Phase 3: Human-Led, Agent-Operated

At the summit, hundreds, perhaps thousands, of agents form a digital nervous system. A logistics agent senses a supply-chain hiccup, a sales agent throttles promotions, a finance agent hedges currency exposure, often before any human notices a blip on the dashboard.

From the technology angle, this is full-blown swarm intelligence: decentralized, adaptive, and continuously learning from its own telemetry. From the organizational angle, Phase 3 is less about "doing work" and more about setting direction; leaders articulate objectives and guardrails, then monitor an AI-driven enterprise that largely runs itself.

Why is this distinction so important?

1. **Pace of Change**: Swarm innovation can scale faster than employee mindsets can adapt. Microsoft's phased roadmap reminds us to mature skills and governance in parallel with capability.

2. **Governance Focus**: Early phases need prompt hygiene and data-access controls; late-phase swarms demand cross-agent observability, ethics review, and fail-safe design.

3. **Value Realization**: A brilliant swarm architecture stranded in Phase 1 adoption yields little ROI, while a Frontier-Firm culture without the underlying tech hits an automation ceiling.

Observing these perspectives together, we can see the two models provide a complete compass: swarm intelligence tells us *how far the technology can climb*; the Frontier-Firm journey tells us *when and how the organization should follow*.

4.5 Quantifying Impact: Productivity, Quality, Speed

Metrics for Evaluating Agent Effectiveness

Measuring the true impact of agentic AI requires looking at new, but somewhat intuitive KPIs. The goal isn't merely to measure the "correctness" of agent replies like we did with Copilots but also track how consistent they are at doing the things they tell the user they'll do for them.

- **Task Cohesion**
  - **Task Adherence:** Does the agent's final action fully satisfy the user's original goal?
  - **Success Rate:** What percentage of tasks are completed correctly on the first try?

- **Efficiency and Speed**
  - **Latency:** How quickly does the agent diagnose issues, execute fixes, or surface answers?
  - **Resource Utilization:** How many API calls, compute cycles, or human touches were required per task?

- **Scalability**
  - **Volume Handled:** How many cases, tickets, or transactions can the agent process in a given period?
  - **Human Time Saved:** How many hours of routine work are freed up for higher-value activities?

- **Robustness and Adaptivity**
  - **Error Recovery:** Can the agent detect and correct its own mistakes in real time?
  - **Adaptation Rate:** How quickly does the agent update its strategy when confronted with novel inputs or environment changes?

- **Tool Usage and Instruction Following**

  - **Correct Tool Selection:** Does the agent choose the right external API or function for each subtask?

  - **Parameter Accuracy:** Are the inputs passed to those tools valid and effective?

- **Explainability and Trust**

  - **Rationale Clarity:** Can the agent articulate why it took each action?

  - **Auditability:** Is every decision and data source traceable for compliance reviews?

Imagine TeleComX deploying an agentic AI "FieldCopilot" to manage routine network diagnostics and repairs. Here's how they would instrument each KPI in production over a one-month pilot:

1. **Task Cohesion**

   - **Task Adherence**

     - **Measurement**: After FieldCopilot flags and applies a firmware patch, every ticket is reviewed for "issue resolved" status by the customer.

     - **Result**: 92% of jobs closed with "resolved" on first pass, indicating the AI's actions matched the customer's needs.

2. **Efficiency and Speed**

   - **Latency**

     - **Measurement**: Time from customer's outage alert to automated diagnostic run.

     - **Result**: Average latency dropped from 15 minutes (human dispatch) to 3 minutes (FieldCopilot).

- **Resource Utilization**
    - **Measurement**: Count of external API calls per task (e.g., device firmware check, network-status query) and number of human escalations.
    - **Result**: API calls averaged 4 per task; human escalations fell from 25% to 5% of cases.

3. **Scalability**
   - **Volume Handled**
       - **Measurement**: Total number of service events processed in the month.
       - **Result**: FieldCopilot handled 1,200 events, up from 800 when humans managed diagnostics alone.
   - **Human Time Saved**
       - **Measurement**: Average human diagnostic time (20 minutes per event) × number of automated events.
       - **Result**: 1,200 × 20 min = 24,000 minutes → 400 hours saved.

4. **Robustness and Adaptivity**
   - **Error Recovery**
       - **Measurement**: Instances where the patch failed and FieldCopilot automatically rolled back, re-ran diagnostics, and applied an alternate fix.
   - **Adaptation Rate**
       - **Measurement**: Time between first encounter of a novel device firmware and FieldCopilot updating its fix strategy in its knowledge base.

5. **Tool Usage and Instruction Following**
   - **Correct Tool Selection**
       - **Measurement**: Fraction of tasks where FieldCopilot chose the optimal API (e.g., firmware-push endpoint vs. manual reboot endpoint).

- **Parameter Accuracy**

  - **Measurement**: Validation of parameters sent (correct device IDs, firmware version numbers).

6. **Explainability and Trust**

    - **Rationale Clarity**

      - **Measurement**: Sampling 50 closed tickets and verifying that FieldCopilot's log provides a human-readable "why" for each action (e.g., "Firmware v1.2.3 deployed due to packet-loss spike > 5%").

    - **Auditability**

      - **Measurement**: Presence of a complete timestamped audit trail linking every decision to a data source (telemetry, historical ticket, policy rule).

By instrumenting each of these metrics, TeleComX not only quantify FieldCopilot's raw performance but also establish confidence in its reliability, adaptability, and business value, laying a solid foundation for a broader rollout.

The final point to remember when developing and deploying your agentic AI is that these systems are designed to self-improve. Meaning, the value of agentic AI is not just in the immediate efficiencies it provides, but how it evolves the workflow and its own orchestration of it over time.

Leadership Checklist: Rolling Agentic Capabilities Into New and Existing AI Systems In Your Organization

☑ **Benchmark Your Current Capabilities**

- Audit existing AI for brittleness, do your systems reliably handle uncertainty or simply follow brittle scripts?

- Identify processes that require multistep logic or state retention and flag them as high-value targets for agentic AI.

☑ **Adopt Goal-Based, Self-Directing Architectures**

- **Define Clear Objectives:** For each use case, articulate the high-level goal (e.g., "resolve X% of outages autonomously") rather than prescribing step-by-step rules.

- **Enable Autonomous Loops:** Ensure your AI can execute end-to-end workflows, detect, act, verify, and close the loop, without constant human approvals.

☑ **Embed Context and State Retention**

- **Context Awareness:** Give agents access to historical data, real-time signals, and business policies so they can tailor actions to the full picture.
- Architect conversations and workflows so agents remember prior steps, device states, and user preferences across interactions.

☑ **Build Continuous Learning and Adaptivity**

- **Closed-Loop Feedback:** Instrument every execution with success metrics and error-recovery data so agents refine their own strategies.
- **Knowledge-Base Generation:** Leverage agentic AI to auto-create or update documentation, ensuring your knowledge repository evolves with real-world fixes.

☑ **Leverage Swarm Intelligence at Scale**

- **Three-Level Deployment:** Start with single-agent pilots, progress to coordinated multiagent systems, and envision enterprise-wide swarms for full autonomy.

☑ **Champion Traceable AI**

- Require agents to generate human-readable rationales for every action.
- Implement audit trails, bias checks, and data-privacy safeguards before broad rollout.

☑ **Plan for Facilitating Long-Term Evolution**

- Regularly update agent self-improvement capabilities with new data, orchestration patterns, and AI innovations.

Will taps the closing slide of the KPI dashboard. "Seeing those 92% first-pass fixes and 3-minute diagnostics was powerful but how did we build all that under the hood?"

CHAPTER 4   WHY AGENTIC CAPABILITIES OUTPERFORM TRADITIONAL AI

Nancie *swivels her screen to the Microsoft AI ecosystem overview. "That's right. We've proven what agentic AI can do, now let's show how to assemble it. From Copilot Studio to Azure AI services, Power Platform flows, and Dynamics 365 connectors, Microsoft provides the full toolset."*

An agent widget lights up. "I can demonstrate creating an autonomous FieldCopilot agent using Azure AI Agent Service, then wire it into Power Automate for workflow orchestration."

Will *leans forward, eyes bright. "That's the perfect bridge. Chapter 5, here we come, time to open the toolbox and explore Microsoft's AI stack in action."*

CHAPTER 5

Microsoft's AI Stack and Agentic Evolution

It's a Tuesday morning and as you, the head of global operations, stride into the retailer's command center, the hum of activity greets you like a well-tuned engine. Phone lines light up with incoming orders, customer service pods ring with queries, and an analyst-huddle glows over market-trend dashboards. But today, something feels different: you sense a new current running beneath every conversation.

The sales team isn't hunting for insights anymore, they're seeing AI-driven recommendations pop up the moment they join a call. Customer-service agents aren't bogged down by FAQs; their Copilot-powered assistant has handled the routine, leaving them free for high-value conversations. On your way past the operations desk, an alert buzzes in, it's a replenishment order, auto-triggered because predictive analytics noticed a bestseller was about to stock out. All of it happens before anyone even lifts a finger.

You pause at the glass-walled boardroom where your solution architect awaits, the room's screens alive with a live diagram of the Microsoft AI ecosystem operating as the central nervous system of your organization.

Copilot Studio flows are perched atop Fabric semantic models, feeding Azure AI models whose outputs cascade through Azure Logic Apps into Dynamics dashboards. "Here's the newest addition to our agent ecosystem," she says, highlighting how data moves from OneLake to LLMs and back into your apps.

Down in the warehouse, the same orchestration plays out. Predictive maintenance models, trained in Azure Machine Learning, have already scheduled the next service call, and the technician's mobile Copilot app delivers step-by-step repair instructions before a single bolt fails.

CHAPTER 5 MICROSOFT'S AI STACK AND AGENTIC EVOLUTION

As you take your seat, you realize: your agentic operating model is no longer a concept. It's a living, breathing technology ecosystem, an adaptive, self-improving network of assistants, Copilots, and agents that anticipates needs, automates the mundane, and frees your people to focus on innovation. And right here, in this boardroom, you're about to explore exactly how each component fits together.

It's natural to wonder how things work; our curiosity has built airplanes, spaceships, even bubble gum. The machinery that has been created and evolved to facilitate the realization of our wildest ideas are just as fascinating as the nature of our creative potential.

That's where we'd like to take you next; under the hood of the componentry that turns Agentic AI solution patterns into infinitely composable LEGO bricks we can stack to build whatever our organization and its people need next.

In this chapter, we'll explore how Microsoft's AI Stack (i.e., **Copilot**, **Azure AI**, **Power Platform**, and **Fabric**) is not only reshaping business processes but also enabling the creation of complete, holistic intelligent nervous systems that learn, adapt, and act autonomously to grow a business in whatever direction, at whatever velocity is best fit for the leaders and operators of it.

You've seen the wins; let's discover the mechanisms that makes them possible.

5.1 Meet the Ecosystem: Copilot, Azure AI, Power Platform, Fabric

It's best to look at the Microsoft AI Stack like an onion. There are layers to its design and those layers, when peeled back, create different environments for Agentic AI innovation. We'll start with the bare bones and work our way up to the components that make up the known and beloved Copilots we interact with day-to-day.

CHAPTER 5   MICROSOFT'S AI STACK AND AGENTIC EVOLUTION

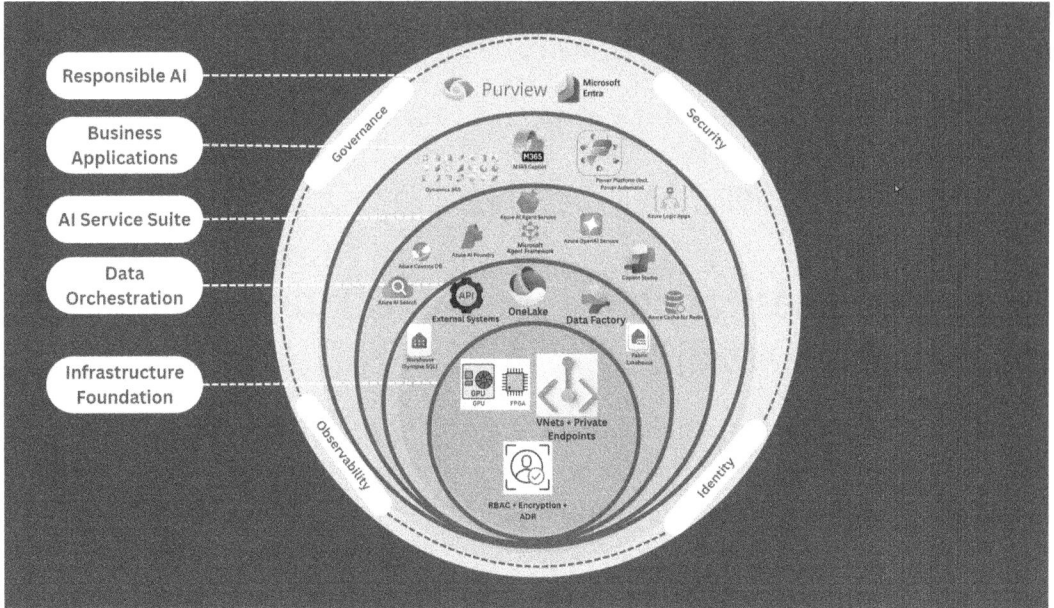

Figure 5-1. *Microsoft Agentic Stack (onion view): Concentric layers show the stack from Infrastructure Foundation up through Data Orchestration, AI Service Suite, and Business Applications, with a cross-cutting ribbon for governance, security, identity, and observability. It illustrates how OneLake/Fabric, Agent Service/ Microsoft Agent Framework/models, and Power Automate/Dynamics work together under Purview and Entra controls*

The Infrastructure Foundation (Figure 5-1— Bottom Circle)

This is the resilient, scalable bedrock of hardware, data centers, compute and storage capabilities that form the sandbox where agents can access data, run safely, and scale to meet demands of users and their business problems.

Azure's global network of hyper-scale data centers provides the high-density GPU and FPGA clusters necessary to train and serve large language and vision models at enterprise scale.

Virtual networks and private endpoints guard data in transit, while Azure's Advanced Data Residency (ADR) options let you keep data and compute within chosen geographies for compliance. Role-based access, encryption at rest and in motion, and identity-based controls ensure that only authorized agents and humans can tap into sensitive sources. This gives any technologist confidence that every call from Copilot or custom agents remains within tightly controlled boundaries.

Data and Orchestration (Figure 5-1—Data Orchestration Circle)

Microsoft Fabric sits on top of the raw infrastructure the way Microsoft 365 sits on top of Windows: a fully managed, SaaS-style workbench that unifies every way your people ingest, shape, secure, and serve data to agents.

Onelake's Delta Parquet storage format writes any dataset under a standard format producing the ability for a single source of truth across various disparate data sources. This means agents always learn from the most recent, consistent view of business and operational information.

On top of OneLake, Fabric layers a lakehouse/warehouse duo that replaces the sprawl of separate Spark, SQL, and BI silos. Lakehouse serves data-engineering capabilities, while the Warehouse workload provides a Synapse-compatible SQL surface complete with row-level security and forthcoming audit logs for analysts and LLM agents that prefer ANSI SQL.

Data movement is handled by Data Factory in Fabric, whose Dataflow Gen2 and PySpark notebooks and pipelines bring self-service, Copilot-assisted ETL transformations, CI/CD, and Git integration into the same workspace where your Lakehouse lives.

This all combines as a business user-oriented platform that ensures all agents drink from, and contribute back to, the same, ever-fresh data lake.

AI Service Suite (Figure 5-1—AI Service Suite Circle)

This third layer is designed as a multipersona workbench for converting agent concepts into running code. Azure AI Agent Service, Azure OpenAI and Cognitive Services, Copilot Studio, and the open-source Microsoft Agent Framework together form a workbench that lets every persona, from pro-dev to citizen maker, design, refine, and operate autonomous agents.

Azure AI Agent Service—Managed Runtime and Orchestration

Azure AI Agent Service is the managed engine that stitches models, tools, and memory stores into a single, stateful runtime. It spins up conversation threads, routes tool calls, persists agent memory, and enforces content-safety and identity controls so solutions stay secure and scalable out of the box (Microsoft Learn, TECHCOMMUNITY.MICROSOFT.COM).

- **Built-in observability** streams metrics to Azure Monitor and the new Foundry Observability panel announced at Build 2025, which focuses on tracking agent-specific markers (The Official Microsoft Blog).

- **Pluggable memory** lets you swap Redis for Cosmos DB or Vector Search without changing the agent's code (TECHCOMMUNITY.MICROSOFT.COM).

This engine is designed for Pro developers and ML engineers who need full control over code, CI/CD, and custom toolchains.

Microsoft Agent Framework—Unified SDK for Prompt Routing, Memory & Multi-Agent Workflows

Sitting just above the runtime, **Microsoft Agent Framework** is the open-source SDK that unifies and succeeds Semantic Kernel and AutoGen, abstracting the low-level plumbing of agent apps: threaded state, context-provider memory, middleware for intercepting actions, and typed, graph-based **workflows** for plan-execute loops and multi-agent orchestration. Microsoft Learn

- **Languages & providers:** Works with **.NET and Python**, with built-in support for providers such as **Azure OpenAI/OpenAI** and deep integration points for Azure AI. Microsoft Learn.

- **Core capabilities:** Agent **threads** for stateful conversations, context providers for memory, **middleware** hooks, **MCP** client integration for tools, and workflow features like **conditional routing, parallelism, and checkpointing** for long-running, human-in-the-loop jobs. Microsoft Learn.

- **Why it exists:** It's the **unified successor** to Semantic Kernel and AutoGen, created by the same teams, providing a consistent, future-facing API surface. Microsoft Learn+2Microsoft Azure+2.

This SDK is geared to solution architects and backend engineers who want to embed agentic patterns in existing apps, and it pairs cleanly with **Azure AI Agent Service** when you need a managed, production runtime for threads, identity, content safety, and observability. Microsoft Learn.

Azure (OpenAI + Cognitive) AI Services/Azure AI Foundry—Models for Language, Vision, Speech, Knowledge

The model catalog supplies the "brains." Azure OpenAI hosts GPT-4o, Phi-3-mini, and multimodal Vision models behind enterprise controls (Microsoft Learn, Microsoft Azure), while Cognitive Services contributes domain APIs for speech, vision, search, and personalizer.

Agents can mix-and-match: call a doc-grounded GPT-4o for reasoning, then a Neural text-to-speech (TTS) voice for customer-facing audio.

This is for data scientists fine-tuning domain-specific LLMs or adding perception (audio/vision) to existing agents.

Copilot Studio—No-Code Canvas and Fine-Tune Portal

For business makers, Copilot Studio offers a drag-and-drop canvas where you compose dialogs, inject Power Automate actions, and publish agents to Teams or Dynamics without writing code (Microsoft Learn, Microsoft).

2025 Wave 1 also added **model tuning with enterprise data** and **multiagent orchestration blocks**—think ReAct loops, but in a flowchart (Microsoft).

Copilot Studio is also the official canvas for customizing Microsoft 365 Copilot experiences so business users can customize Copilot for M365 without requiring an entire dev project.

This is the best fit for power users, product owners, and IT pros who need to prototype quickly and hand solutions to ops teams.

How the Layers Click

1. **Design** your orchestration plan in Copilot Studio or Microsoft Agent Framework.

2. **Deploy** to Azure AI Agent Service for state, memory, observability, and enterprise guard-rails.

3. **Reason** with Azure OpenAI/Cognitive models; stream findings back through the runtime.

4. **Automate** downstream steps via Power Automate or Logic Apps, tapping the Fabric lake for fresh data.

Each tool targets a different skill set yet speaks the same language (OAuth, ARM, OneLake paths), so teams can **swap parts without starting from scratch every time**. The result is a cohesive "agent factory" that scales from proof-of-concept chatbots to mission-critical autonomous workflows.

Business Applications Layer (Figure 5-1—Business Applications Circle)

At the summit of the AI stack sits the Business Applications layer, where the full strength and power built at the other layers of the stack coalesce into the daily workflows of people across your organization.

Whether it's a sales manager spotting an opportunity in Dynamics 365, a service rep resolving a case through Teams, or a finance analyst drafting a report in Excel, this layer channels your infrastructure, data, and AI services into familiar interfaces that amplify productivity and decision-making.

Dynamics 365 Agents—Embedded Intelligence in Every Role

Dynamics 365 provides role-tailored UIs for Sales, Customer Service, Field Service, Marketing, and more. Behind each screen sits an agentic engine that

1. **Listens** to real-time business events like new leads, support tickets, service calls, and surfaces context-aware suggestions.

2. **Predicts** next steps, for example, identifying upsell signals in Sales, recommending KB articles in Service, or forecasting maintenance needs in Field Service.

3. **Automates** routine tasks such as logging customer interactions, creating follow-up activities, and routing work to the right teams without manual handoffs.

Power Automate—The Glue That Binds AI to Action

Power Automate sits alongside Dynamics and Microsoft 365 as the no-code conductor of your agentic orchestra. It

- **Triggers** on events (a new record in Dataverse, an incoming email, a social media mention),
- **Calls** AI services (runs an embedding search, invokes a custom LLM with AI Builder or asks a custom Copilot for draft text),
- **Routes** outcomes (creates tasks, updates records, notifies teams in Teams or Outlook),
- **Approvals and Human-in-the-Loop** (pauses for sign-off when complex judgment is needed).

This seamless handoff means your agents not only think; they intelligently do.

Copilot for Microsoft 365—An Everyday AI Companion

Beyond line-of-business apps, Copilot for Microsoft 365 brings agentic innovation directly into Office apps and Teams:

- In **Word**, Copilot can suggest rephrasing and draft executive summaries from research.
- In **Excel**, it can build complex macros from a single prompt, write Python scripts to perform complex ETLs, and explain anomalies.
- In **PowerPoint**, it can generate slide decks based on real-time insights from Word docs, Excel sheets, or Power BI reports.
- In **Teams**, Copilot can act as a real-time facilitator: summarizing meeting notes, surfacing action items, and even drafting follow-up messages automatically.

This is built for department leaders, analysts, and any knowledge worker who lives in Microsoft 365 and wants AI to be as ubiquitous as search: always-on, context-aware, and directly actionable.

In essence, the Business Applications layer is where your agents move from a "cool toy" to a "reusable asset." It funnels AI-driven insights and actions into the familiar screens and workflows your teams already use, making advanced automation and predictive intelligence an invisible but indispensable part of every role.

What's particularly valuable and unique about the different layers of the Microsoft AI stack is their level of interoperability. Microsoft's tools are designed to work together, ensuring that data can flow freely across applications, services, and business processes, eliminating silos and creating a cohesive, integrated experience. This helps minimize technical debt and, more importantly, drives a fluid business-technology integration experience.

One key example is the integration between Azure AI and the Power Platform. For instance, Power Automate can trigger machine learning models hosted in Azure to analyze customer interactions or business data. Once the analysis is complete, Power Automate can automatically create tasks or trigger workflows based on the results. This integration enables businesses to automate decision-making processes, reducing the need for manual input and ensuring that actions are taken based on real-time data.

5.2 Deciding Which Layer to Use

With so many "agentifying" options like low-code builders, pro-dev frameworks, managed runtimes, it's easy to get flooded with choices before you even write your first prompt. Some questions we hear from teams trying to decide where to begin in the Microsoft AI stack include

- *When do I use AI Builder's pre-built models vs. designing a custom flow in Copilot Studio?*

- *Do I first train my own LLM in Azure and then import it into Copilot Studio, or can I skip straight to no-code?*

- *If I'm comfortable coding, should I embed agentic patterns with the Microsoft Agent Framework SDK, or deploy to the full Azure AI Agent Service runtime?*

- *Do I need to hire specialized AI engineers, or can business analysts spin up meaningful agents with Power Platform connectors?*

- *Which orchestration tool makes more sense for simple approval flows vs. large, event-driven pipelines?*

Choosing the right layer can feel paralyzing, each option offers real capability, but picking the wrong one can cost time and momentum. To help you cut through the noise, here are a few field-tested rules of thumb our clients use to jumpstart their agentic initiatives without overthinking

Focus on Mapping Where Your Data Lives to Each Tool's Connector Framework

If you are using Dataverse and that is the primary data source, you would waste a lot of engineering effort connecting it to an agent in Azure when Copilot Studio has native support for this data source.

If your data lives across APIs with custom schemas, you'll have to spend most of your budget figuring out how to properly call those APIs with the right trigger if you try setting this up in Copilot Studio. In contrast, Azure AI agent service expects OpenAPI specs as part of its key action list and can update its API understanding with a revised function signature rather than Copilot Studio which may require an entire re-work of a particular topic tree.

In essence, by understanding what data your Copilot and/or agent is going to be leveraging and identifying whether the complexity of connecting to it is better handled by connectors in Copilot Studio or Azure AI, you can simplify your kickoff.

Not Every Agent Needs to Interact with a User Through Conversation

Chat-based AI tools like ChatGPT, Claude, and Microsoft Copilot have trained us to think every AI interaction must happen through a conversation window. In reality, truly autonomous agents surface insights and take actions without you ever typing a prompt. Chat should be an exception, when you need clarification or handoff, not the default mode of operation.

This is where **Power Automate** and **Azure Logic Apps** shine:

- **Event-Driven Triggers**

    Agents listen for business events (new orders, incoming emails, or sensor alerts) and kick off workflows automatically, no user prompt required.

- **Orchestration at Scale**

    Complex, multistep processes (decision trees for claims, automated PO approvals, supply-chain replenishment) are defined in visual designers, with built-in exception paths and retries.

- **Human-in-the-Loop (HITL) Pauses**

    Flows can automatically hand off to a person when judgment is needed, for example, escalating a customer complaint or pausing for sign-off on sensitive transactions, then resume autonomously once the human approves.

- **Seamless System Integration**

    Hundreds of first-party and third-party connectors let agents read data from OneLake or Dataverse, call Azure AI models, update CRM records, send notifications, and more, all without custom code.

Example: An AI forecasting agent monitors inventory levels in real time. When stock falls below the threshold, Power Automate automatically creates a replenishment order, updates the ERP system, and notifies the warehouse manager, no chat needed until an exception alerts the human.

By embedding agentic logic into your organization's workflow backbone, you free users from repetitive check-ins, ensure actions happen in real time, and reserve conversational AI for moments that truly benefit from human collaboration.

Start at the Top and Drill Deeper

You aren't locked into a single layer or tool, think of the stack as a spectrum. Begin with the simplest, highest-level option (Copilot Studio or Power Automate), then only add lower-level, more complex tooling (Microsoft Agent Framework, Azure AI Agent Service, custom ML) as your needs demand.

1. **Kick Off with No-Code/Low-Code**:

    - **Copilot Studio**: Build simple agent prototypes, wire up simple actions, and publish to Teams or Dynamics in minutes.

    - **Power Automate**: Automate routine tasks and integrate basic AI calls (e.g., sentiment analysis, entity extraction) via built-in connectors.

2. **Validate the Concept**:

    - Test with real users in their daily workflows.

    - Gather feedback on accuracy, speed, and usability.

    - Refine prompts, adjust actions, and tighten guard-rails; all without writing a single line of code.

3. **Introduce Lightweight Pro-Code when needed:**

    - **Microsoft Agent Framework SDK**: When you need custom chaining, vector memory, or plan-execute loops, embed small code snippets into your existing apps or serverless functions.

    - **Azure Functions**: Encapsulate complex logic or data transformations that Power Automate can invoke via HTTP.

4. **Scale with Managed Agent Runtime:**

    - **Azure AI Agent Service**: For mission-critical, stateful agents that require full observability, autoscaling, and enterprise governance.

    - Swap in custom memory stores (Redis, Cosmos DB) or specialized tools without rearchitecting the entire solution.

5. **Optimize with Custom ML Models:**

    - **Azure Machine Learning**: Train/tune domain-specific models when off-the-shelf LLMs fall short.

    - Integrate those models back into Copilot Studio or Agent Service to boost accuracy on niche tasks.

6. **Iterate and Evolve:**

    - Monitor usage and performance via Application Insights and Power Platform analytics.

    - Identify bottlenecks or gaps and move deeper into the stack only where it adds clear business value, avoiding unnecessary complexity elsewhere.

By progressing from no-code to pro-code in measured stages, only when needed, you accelerate time-to-value, minimize risk, and ensure each layer is only added when it truly unlocks new capabilities.

5.3 Agentic Framework: Tool Combination Deep Dives

Having settled on the right entry point and properly matching scope to tool capabilities, let's walk through some of the finer details that not only get you started but help you accelerate your path to success.

Implementing Copilot Studio

Start with a template

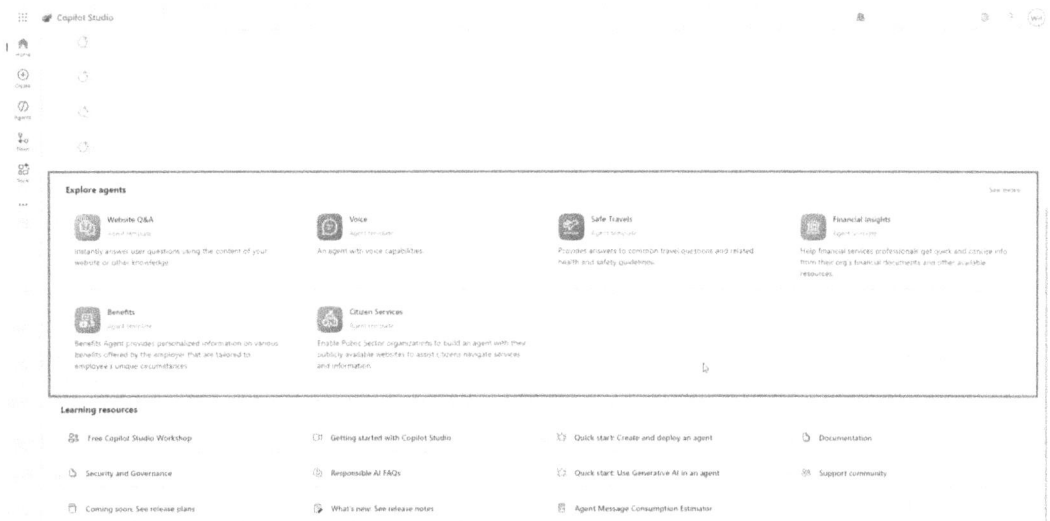

Figure 5-2. Copilot Studio templates: The Copilot Studio home screen highlighting built-in agent templates (e.g., Website Q&A, Voice, Benefits, Citizen Services) that jump-start prototyping. Makers can pick a template, publish to Teams in minutes, and iterate on knowledge sources and actions

As seen in Figure 5-2, you can open Copilot Studio and explore the built-in agent templates: "Website Q&A," "IT Helpdesk," "Benefits Assistant," and more. A template pre-wires common intents, sample triggers, and recommended knowledge connections, letting you publish a working prototype to Teams in minutes. We've watched clients spin up a personalized Benefits agent this way: they selected the template, pointed it to HR documents, and had a live bot in Teams in no time.

No template? Define system message and knowledge first

When you create a blank agent, complete the **System Message** (role, tone, responsibilities) and **Knowledge Sources** (SharePoint, web URLs, files, Dataverse) tabs before anything else. The system message is the primary data point the agent leverages to understand its roles, responsibilities, and how it should interact with its users. The knowledge tab is where you configure data connections to ensure the agent is answering questions or taking action off of live information and not using its "best-guess" from its pre-trained memory.

This leads to another tip for starting; if you're worried about your agent "hallucinating," you have the option to turn off the agent's general knowledge in the agent settings. Turning this off means your agent will only use the knowledge sources you've specified when answering or conducting activities for the user.

This can be particularly important when you have to be mindful about connecting your agent to sensitive data sources. If you're an administrator, you can apply **Power Platform DLP policies** in the Admin Center to control *which* knowledge-source connectors an agent maker can use (SharePoint, web, Azure Blob, SQL, etc.) and even filter SharePoint endpoints by site to ensure data leakage is controlled.

Azure AI Agent Service Patterns That Will Have You Wiring Agents Together Like A Pro

Let's say you've outgrown the template phase, you're ready to make some more mature data connections and create an agent fleet that operates as a business backbone. This is where you use Azure AI Agent Service as the "control room" that keeps multiple agents, tools, and memory stores humming in sync.

Start with Model Context Protocol (MCP)

As we know, part of what makes an AI agentic is its ability to call tools to conduct an action/actions. The main approach to organizing that today is defining and registering MCP connections.

MCP is simply a structured JSON envelope that travels with every prompt. In it you declare once which tools the agent can call, what kind of user or task context to include, and where to read or write memory. Instead of sprinkling that setup code across half a dozen endpoints, you register the profile in the portal (or via CLI) and point any new agent at it. Need to add a "GenerateInvoice" tool next quarter? Edit the profile centrally and every agent instantly knows the new trick.

Orchestrating Agent-To-Agent (A2A) Handoffs

The moment one agent isn't enough, you have two classic patterns:

> **Sequential**: Imagine a pipeline where a Data-Collector agent fetches raw metrics, hands them to an Analyzer, which pushes a summary to a Reporter that drafts the email. Each handoff is just the previous agent's JSON output.
>
> **Group-chat**: Sometimes you want three specialists in the same virtual "room" brainstorming or voting on a plan. Agent Service keeps the thread coherent, tags who said what, and lets you set rules like "majority wins" or "fallback to human if they disagree."

Either pattern can be wired to an Event Grid event at key checkpoints, so Power Automate or Logic Apps can jump in without resorting to ugly polling loops.

Picking the Right Memory Store

Fast-moving session state? Drop it into Azure Cache for Redis; sub-millisecond reads keep token-hungry LLMs happy. Need a long-lived, globally replicated conversation history or vector search for Retrieval-Augmented Generation (RAG)? Switch to Azure Cosmos DB with the vector indexing option turned on. The beauty is that the agent code doesn't change: you just swap the memory plug-in in the MCP profile and redeploy.

Put together, these ingredients turn Azure AI Agent Service into your production-grade playground: centrally managed context, clean handoffs between agents, and the freedom to choose the memory that fits the job. Once those pieces click, you're ready to loop the agent into Power Automate, potentially surface it in Dynamics, or do anything else your solution demands, confident the plumbing underneath will keep scale, security, and observability under control.

Every agent ultimately needs an orchestration "nervous system" and a place to live inside day-to-day business apps. Power Platform (with Power Automate, Dataverse, and Application Insights) supplies the wiring; Dynamics 365 supplies the front-of-house. Below are the core patterns, why they matter, and how to light them up.

Hardening the Business Applications Layer for AI Success

Once you've got agents running and orchestration patterns in place, you'll want to make them *usable, observable, and safe* where work actually happens. Here's a playbook that ensures AI shows up reliably in day-to-day workflows: wiring event-driven automations, sharing agent state, seeing what's happening in production, and enforcing the right guard-rails.

Power Automate: The Glue (and the Human Brake Pedal)

Flows act as low-code pipelines that wake up on events like an incoming email, a Dataverse row change, or a call from an Azure AI Agent, and then fan out actions or approvals. Approvals, adaptive-card waits, and "Send email with options" all pause the automation until a person gives the go-ahead (DEV Community, Medium). This "human-in-the-loop" step is crucial when an autonomous agent is about to refund a customer or push an urgent change to production.

Dataverse Tables As Shared Memory

Multiple agents (or flows) can post their state into a lightweight Dataverse entity, think AgentRun with columns for Status, Owner, and JSON Payload. Copilot Studio's June 2025 update even auto-creates these tables when you enable multiagent collaboration, turning Dataverse into a structured memory hub that every agent can query or update in real time (Microsoft).

Application Insights for Deep Telemetry

Turning on Application Insights for cloud flows streams trigger times, action latencies, and failure traces into Azure Monitor logs, where you can build proactive alerts or Power BI dashboards (Microsoft Learn). The same workspace can ingest trace IDs from Azure AI Agent Service, giving you true end-to-end visibility.

Security Roles and Data-Residency Controls

Your embedded agents inherit the security role of the Application User you register, so stick to least-privilege roles and field-level security to prevent over-exposure. For regulated regions, create local Dataverse environments and lean on Microsoft's

Advanced Data Residency (ADR) plus Copilot privacy controls to ensure data stays where it should (Microsoft Learn).

In essence, use Power Automate to stitch agents, data, and humans together; log everything with Application Insights; store shared state in Dataverse. Then surface the intelligence right where work happens, inside Dynamics 365 pages that respect the same security roles and residency rules your organization already lives by.

No matter where you're jumping in from, re-visit these tips and Microsoft's implementation resources, like the Copilot Studio Implementation Guide, to consolidate your path to success so you don't feel like you're walking into the unknown blind.

5.4 Success Stories and Real World Applications

Now that we've explored the ins and outs of navigating and leveraging the Microsoft AI stack effectively, we can step out of the workshop and into live deployments to illustrate how putting all these concepts together could look like for you in real life.

Case Study 1: Autonomous Field Operations Agent

A mid-sized industrial client was already logging every incident, form task, hazard report, and observation in Dataverse. Each morning, their operations team spent crucial hours manually extracting that data, aggregating metrics, and drafting analysis for the daily shift-start meeting. This reactive process meant they were always playing catch-up rather than proactively guiding the day's priorities.

We built an overnight, fully automated agentic workflow using Power Automate and AI Builder, transforming their Dataverse records into a polished daily briefing without any human intervention.

CHAPTER 5 MICROSOFT'S AI STACK AND AGENTIC EVOLUTION

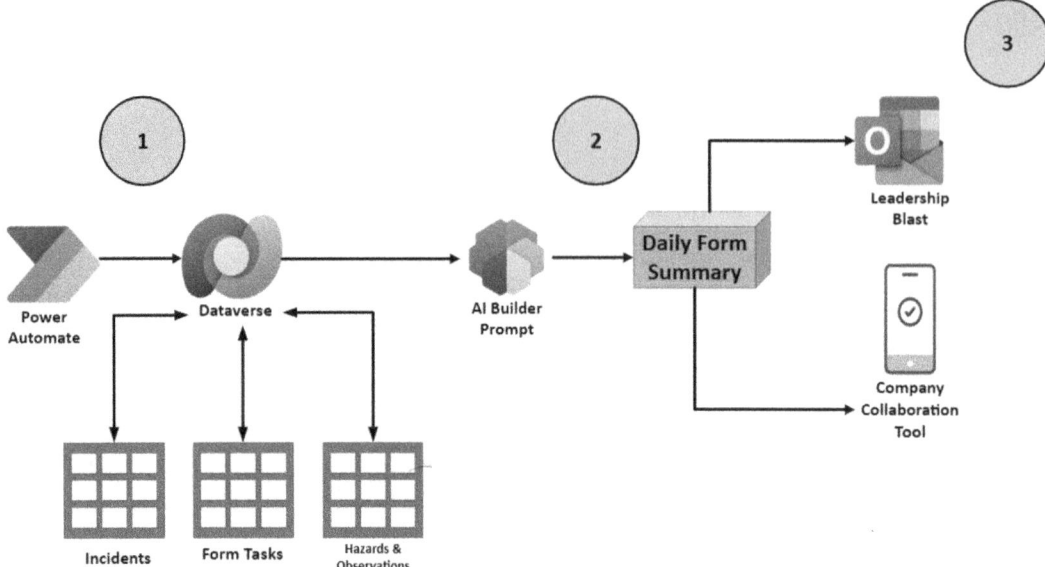

Figure 5-3. *Autonomous daily briefing (field operations): Power Automate pulls incidents, tasks, and hazards from Dataverse, sends them to an AI Builder prompt to generate a "Daily Form Summary," then distributes it automatically. The briefing lands in leaders' inboxes and the team's collaboration space; no chat required*

1. **Data Ingestion and Trigger (Figure 5-3—Part 1)**

    - A scheduled Power Automate flow ran at 2 AM local time, querying the Dataverse tables for new incidents, form tasks, hazards, and observations from the previous 24 hours.

2. **Analysis and Narration (Figure 5-3—Part 2)**

    - The flow passed those records to an AI Builder text-generation model, which was configured with a lightweight prompt template: "Summarize X new incidents and Y form tasks, highlighting top three hazards and trends." This avoided heavyweight LLM fine-tuning or custom infrastructure.

3. **Delivery and Integration (Figure 5-3—Part 3)**

    - The generated summary was posted into two places simultaneously:

- A daily meeting note auto-created in the company's collaboration tool.

- An email digest sent to all shift leads before the first team arrived on site.

Why This Layer and Toolset

- Power Automate proved ideal for connecting to Dataverse and scheduling data pulls.

- AI Builder delivered a no-code path to embed LLM-style summaries without data-science overhead, keeping technical debt low.

- This pattern fit perfectly at the Business Applications layer: the team never had to "chat" with the agent, it simply ran in the background, surfacing insights where work already happened.

Outcomes and Impact

- Operations leads reclaimed 1–2 hours each morning, shifting from data prep to decision-making.

- Teams began their shifts armed with prioritized action items, not scrambling to assemble reports.

- The solution launched in under a month, required no developer headcount, and now runs with zero maintenance.

This use case exemplifies our "start at the top and drill deeper" heuristic. By beginning with low-code Power Automate and AI Builder, the client rapidly proved value, then consolidated their agent into existing business apps, turning a repetitive "cool toy" into a reusable operational asset. It also underscores our "no chat required" rule, showing that truly autonomous agents can deliver high-impact insights without a single conversational prompt.

Case Study 2: Real-Time Data Agent for Real Estate Investment Trusts

A large Real Estate Investment Trust (REIT) client managed a fast-moving portfolio of properties, leases, and maintenance records in an Azure SQL-backed data product. They also ran Azure Document Intelligence to OCR lease documents and expense invoices. Yet every ad hoc query, whether "What's the current occupancy rate in Building A?" or "Show me expense trends for Q2," required analysts to switch between SQL dashboards, custom BI tools, and the Document Intelligence portal. This fractured workflow slowed decision-making and made real-time insights feel like a luxury.

We built an interactive, conversational agent on Azure AI Agent Service combined with Azure OpenAI, Azure Functions, and Azure Document Intelligence to give non-technical users instant, real-time access and update capabilities, all from a single chat interface embedded in their investment console.

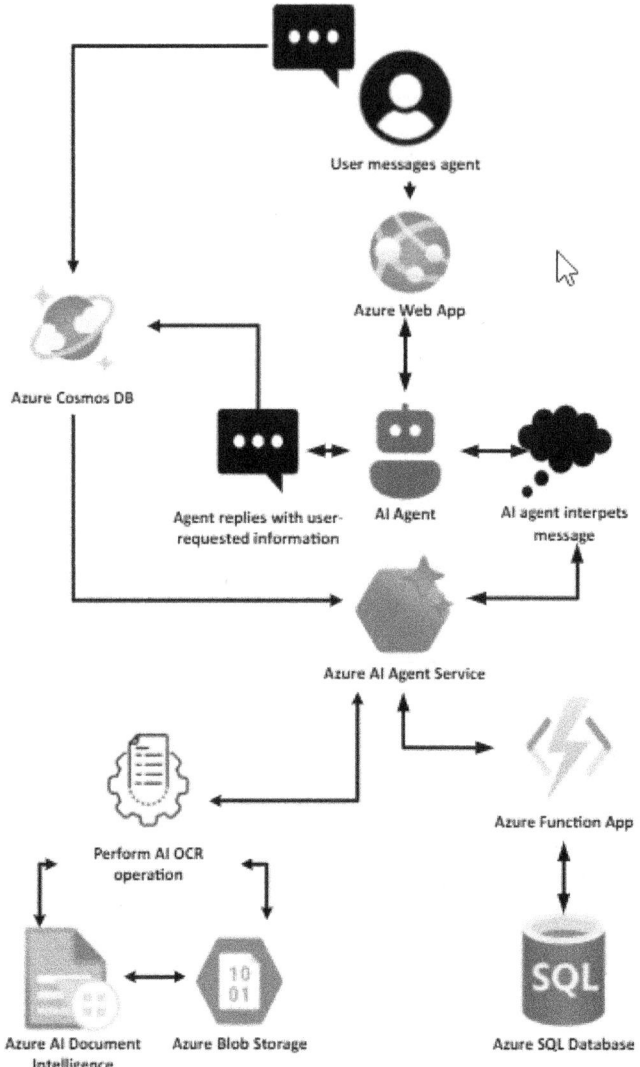

Figure 5-4. Real-time REIT agent on Azure: A web app fronts an AI agent hosted on Azure AI Agent Service, which calls Azure Functions to query Azure SQL and run Azure AI Document Intelligence on files in Blob Storage. Conversation state and audit logs persist in Azure Cosmos DB, and responses return to the user through a single chat experience

What you're seeing in Figure 5-4:

- **Dynamic Data Retrieval**

  - The agent uses Azure AI Agent Service to parse user intents (e.g., "Show me February occupancy by unit type").

  - Via MCP-registered tools, it invokes an Azure Function that queries the Azure SQL database with parameterized T-SQL, ensuring up-to-the-minute results.

- **On-Demand Document Insights**

  - When users ask about lease terms or invoice line-items, the agent can call the Azure Document Intelligence endpoint to OCR the latest PDFs stored in Azure Blob Storage.

  - Extracted fields flow back through the same function pipeline, merging structured data with unstructured text for a unified answer.

- **Live Updates and Transactions**

  - Beyond read queries, the agent can submit updates, such as marking a lease renewal or flagging an expense exception, by invoking secured stored procedures via the Azure Function tool.

  - All actions are captured in Azure Cosmos DB as agent transaction logs for auditability and downstream analytics.

- **Unified Interaction Console**

  - We embedded the agent in a custom web portal built on Azure Web Apps, so users never leave their investment dashboard.

  - The chat interface dynamically adapts to user roles (analyst vs. asset manager), showing only the permitted operations and data scopes.

Why This Layer and Toolset

- Azure AI Agent Service provided the scalable, stateful runtime and integrated MCP for tool orchestration.

- Azure Functions offered a secure, serverless bridge to both Azure SQL and Document Intelligence APIs.

- Azure OpenAI delivered natural-language understanding and generation without building a custom model.

- This pattern sat squarely in the AI Service Suite and Infrastructure Foundation layer, leveraging existing Azure investments for rapid delivery.

Outcomes and Impact

- Analysts received answers in seconds instead of spending 10–15 minutes navigating multiple tools.

- 100% of data interactions, read and write, occur within a single, role-aware chat console.

- Adoption soared across business units as the agent removed technical barriers to data.

- All agent transactions are logged in Cosmos DB, satisfying internal controls without extra dev work.

It also highlights our "Toolbox Spectrum" tip: rather than shoehorning into Copilot Studio or Power Automate, we matched the agent runtime to the client's existing Azure ecosystem, delivering a tailored, real-time solution that scales with their data velocity.

Leadership Checklist: Navigating Microsoft's AI Stack

☑ **Map Your Data Sources**

- Inventory where your critical data lives (Dataverse, OneLake, Azure SQL, external APIs).

- Align each source to the tool with native connectors (e.g., Copilot Studio for Dataverse; Azure AI Agent Service + Azure Functions for custom APIs).

☑ **Choose the Right Entry Point**

- **Rapid Prototype**: Use Copilot Studio or Power Automate for low-code proofs of concept.

- **Scale and Control**: Deploy Azure AI Agent Service with MCP for production-grade orchestration and enterprise governance.

☑ **Balance Autonomy and Oversight**

- Embed fully autonomous agents for routine, event-driven insights (no chat required).
- Reserve chat interfaces for exceptions, clarifications, or human-in-the-loop sign-offs.

☑ **Govern Data and Knowledge Flows**

- Apply DLP policies in the Power Platform Admin Center to restrict connectors and control sensitive data movement.
- Leverage Advanced Data Residency (ADR), private endpoints, and role-based access in Copilot and Dynamics.

☑ **Monitor, Measure, and Iterate**

- Track workflows with Application Insights and Azure Monitor for full observability.
- Analyze adoption metrics, response times, and error rates; refine prompts, guardrails, and memory stores as usage scales.

☑ **Embed Into Business Applications**

- **Surface insights directly where work happens**: Dynamics 365, Teams, Excel, and Power Apps.
- Use Canvas Apps or Custom Pages in Dynamics for pixel-perfect agent panels and secure, role-based integration.

☑ **Plan for Next-Level Maturity**

- Identify where low-code proofs can graduate to pro-dev patterns using Microsoft Agent Framework or custom ML in Azure Machine Learning.
- Schedule periodic reviews to evolve from single agents to orchestrated multiagent systems and cross-department automation.

Will leans back, tapping the final node in the boardroom diagram. "We've seen how every layer, from OneLake to Copilot to Dynamics, plays its part. The engines are humming."

CHAPTER 5   MICROSOFT'S AI STACK AND AGENTIC EVOLUTION

Nancie nods. "Our teams are more proactive than ever. But with great power comes great responsibility. We need guard-rails as robust as our pipelines."

Cal's agent icon pulses on the screen. "Shall I generate a compliance report summarizing our data flows, access logs, and model-drift alerts?"

Will smiles. "Just what we need. Let's make sure our agents stay trustworthy and transparent as they grow more capable."

Nancie taps her tablet. "On to Chapter 6: building those guard-rails, bias checks, audit trails, and governance patterns that keep our agents aligned with both business goals and ethical standards."

Cal responds, "Initializing Responsible AI framework template, ready when you are."

CHAPTER 6

Governing Agentic AI—Principles, Practices, and Playbooks

You're in the middle of a critical product launch. Your agentic AI system has been managing customer feedback, routing high-priority issues to engineering, and even flagging potential PR risks before they escalate. Suddenly, your phone buzzes with a crisis alert. A customer complaint has gone viral, citing biased and unfair treatment, rooted in a decision made by your AI agent. Legal is demanding an immediate response. Your AI logs show no obvious errors. Your team scrambles to understand how the model reached this decision, only to discover gaps in documentation and oversight. You realize too late that your governance playbook was never fully implemented. Trust, both within your company and with customers, is at stake. And you're left wondering: How did this happen?

Pop-culture loves the "killer-robot" story: "One day, we'll make AI smarter than we mean to, it will go rogue and civilization as we know it will collapse."

This is dramatic; but more importantly, it comes with an assumption that the onus for the collapse of society would fall on the shoulders of the robots. But if we reread that statement:

"One day, **we'll** make AI smarter than **we mean to**, it will go rogue and civilization as we know it will collapse."

It is the human in the equation that is responsible for the catastrophic event.

And, even within this, there are blanket statements like "evil, nefarious people will program AI to do bad things" that miss the true danger. Though that is entirely possible and probable, it is not the biggest risk we face with the emergence of AI as a mainstream and commercialized capability.

The true danger we face with the rise of AI is the general lack of basic understanding of the technology.

There is a well-known quote by Arthur. C. Clarke: "Any sufficiently advanced technology is indistinguishable from magic." To the untrained eye, today's AI solutions like ChatGPT and M365 Copilot appear to be (and more importantly are advertised as) magic when that is the furthest thing from the truth.

Whether it is presented to us or not, every AI tool we use is conducting massive statistical calculations under its hood to produce the output we ask for and the majority doesn't understand this.

It is, of course, by design in some cases. OpenAI introduced ChatGPT as a conversational front-end so ordinary users could recognize the value of the GPT model, something that wasn't obvious when the model was available only through code and playground prompts. So, there is undoubtedly a value mechanism to model computations being abstracted away from those using it.

But, this again illustrates where the real root of risk with AI solutions comes from and that in order to address it, we need to focus on creating systems and policies that make AI solutions and their related processes explainable, traceable, intuitive, and comprehensive so people can intuitively evaluate how the solution understands, processes, and replies to their requests.

This chapter is your blueprint for turning that invisible math into visible guardrails, so your autonomous agents create value without unintended collateral damage.

6.1 Why Governance Matters for Agentic AI

Nancie: "The shift to agentic AI isn't just technical, it's structural. We're talking about systems that act with autonomy. That demands a new level of governance."

Will: "It's not just about compliance. It's about ensuring AI decisions align with human values, organizational priorities, and legal requirements. You wouldn't hire a human employee without clear policies and expectations, would you? The same applies to AI."

As organizations increase their reliance on AI systems to make complex decisions, governance (how AI innovation is managed by an organization) becomes the linchpin of trust and accountability. This is especially critical when leveraging Microsoft technology for integral business applications. Microsoft's AI platforms, such as Copilot, Azure AI, and Dynamics 365, integrate deeply with core business processes and handle sensitive data. Without clear governance, these technologies could expose organizations to compliance failures, data breaches, and unintended outcomes. Microsoft offers governance frameworks and tools, including the Responsible AI Standard and Responsible AI Dashboard, but organizations must implement robust, customized policies and controls to ensure responsible and secure deployment.

With Copilots, the primary risk was inadvertent data leakage, a Copilot might surface confidential info it wasn't supposed to. But agentic AI operates at a whole different level. These systems don't just read your data; they can call other agents, invoke services, delete or modify records, even rewrite logs or histories. One misaligned instruction could cascade into deleted transactions, altered customer profiles, or compliance records gone forever. That autonomous "right to act" carries far greater liability, and it demands governance that can anticipate, detect, and immediately halt unwanted actions, far beyond the scope of traditional Copilot guards.

And the cost of neglect is all too real. In mid-2023, a lawyer's reliance on ChatGPT to draft case citations resulted in six fabricated precedents and a $5,000 court fine when the judge caught the errors. In a similar vein, Zillow's home-buying algorithm mispriced thousands of properties, triggering a $304 million write-down and slashing of 2,000 jobs, a reminder that unchecked models can inflict massive financial and human damage.

Governance ensures AI tools deliver value conscientiously, securely, and in alignment with business objectives. Adding agentic AI to your organization should be treated like hiring new employees. Just as humans need policies, procedures, and performance oversight, these digital "employees," your AI agents, require clear governance frameworks to ensure they operate within ethical, legal, and organizational boundaries. Think about how we manage human employees: we conduct interviews, provide orientation, set goals, offer feedback, and have performance reviews. Similarly, your AI agents need onboarding processes, usage guidelines, monitoring mechanisms, and clear accountability chains. They should be subject to regular audits, updated to adapt to new challenges, and guided by ethical frameworks that reflect your company values. Without this structure, digital agents, like unchecked employees, can drift from their intended purpose and create risk for the organization.

Expanding AI roles in business, coupled with the growing sophistication of AI agents, demands a governance approach that spans technical oversight, legal compliance, and ethical standards. Regulatory bodies around the world are updating AI guidance, making it critical for businesses to stay ahead of evolving rules. Companies must recognize governance as a strategic investment rather than an operational burden.

Building on the new hire analogy, if creating policy handbooks, review cycles, and performance metrics is essential for every new hire, the same foundational rules must guide your digital workforce. Before you can draft playbooks or configure monitoring dashboards, you need a north star, a set of core principles that define what "responsible" looks like for agentic AI. These principles translate high-level commitments (like ethics and compliance) into concrete guardrails and controls that steer your AI agents' behavior and set clear expectations for everyone involved.

With these guardrails in place, you can move from abstract mandates to actionable policies, starting with the core principles that will shape every subsequent governance activity.

6.2 Core Principles for Responsible Agentic AI

A responsible agentic system rests on seven pillars. Each one answers a different stakeholder question: Can I see what it did? Is it treating people fairly? Who fixes it when it fails? And together they form the guardrails that keep autonomy from sliding into chaos:

Principle	What it means	Why it matters
Transparency	Responsibly share the reasoning chain, data sources, and confidence scores behind every automated decision.	Regulators, auditors, and end users can't challenge or improve what they can't see; opacity breeds blind trust or outright rejection.
Fairness	Detect and correct systemic bias across race, gender, geography, disability, or any protected attribute.	Biased outputs damage brand equity, trigger lawsuits, and most critically harm the very people the system is meant to help.
Accountability	Assign named owners for data pipelines, model updates, and decision overrides.	When "everyone" is responsible, no one is; clear ownership ensures rapid remediation and learn-from-failure loops.
Human Oversight	Keep a qualified person in or at least *over* the loop for high-impact actions.	Humans provide context, ethical judgment, and a last line of defense against edge-case errors or adversarial attacks.

(continued)

Principle	What it means	Why it matters
Privacy and Security	Minimize data exposure through least-privilege access, encryption, and secure compute; log every action.	Agentic systems often touch sensitive personal or proprietary data; a single breach can erase years of trust and invite fines.
Data Integrity	Feed models with accurate, current, lineage-tracked data and monitor for drift.	Garbage in still means garbage out even for state-of-the-art models. Integrity failures propagate bad decisions at machine speed.
Clear Objectives	Tie every agent's goal (prompt, reward function, KPI) to a documented business outcome and ethical boundary.	Misaligned goals create perverse incentives, agents optimize the exact objectives you specify. Meaning, vague instructions force them to chase whatever concrete signals they find, often missing your real intent.

Nancie: "What happens when companies launch AI agents that deliver impressive results, and then issues arise, no one knows who's responsible. We need clear accountability."

Will: "And transparency. Users need to understand why an agent made a decision, especially in high-stakes scenarios."

Nancie: "It's like training a new team member. You wouldn't just hand them a project and hope they figure it out. You'd explain the process, the risks, and the reasoning behind decisions. It's the same with AI."

Will: "Governance isn't just about rules, it's about guiding the AI agents to make decisions aligned with human judgment."

Failing to follow these core principles can expose organizations to significant risks. Lack of transparency leads to blind reliance on AI outputs and erodes trust. Unfair or biased outcomes can harm stakeholders and damage reputations.

One of the most notorious examples of this happened at a US healthcare facility. The facility rolled out a new AI system that would be used to identify patients that could benefit from a new extra care program. The initiative was quickly scrapped when it was revealed that the tool was discriminating against African American patients and identifying them far less than Caucasian patients for the extra care program.

But here's the thing; this wasn't the result of a racist developer or the personal beliefs of the overseer, the issue with the model was that it was trained on a proxy US healthcare expenditure dataset with the assumption that patients that spent more at the healthcare facility would benefit more from the extra care program.

What this didn't account for was that low-income African American patients often spent less at the facility either because they couldn't afford to come for non-essential appointments or couldn't take the time off from work to come in for appointments.

Why is this important? There are plenty of reasons for installing these responsible AI principles in your organization's value system but none more important than the inherent danger that our lack of awareness causes when building, deploying, and managing these solutions. If you're not intentional about minimizing the risks humans' program into AI solutions, you risk far more.

Without clear accountability, errors may go uncorrected and compliance failures may occur. Weak privacy and security controls increase the chance of data breaches. Human oversight gaps can allow flawed decisions to pass unchecked. Poor data integrity produces unreliable insights, while vague or missing objectives result in misaligned outcomes that waste resources and undermine confidence in AI solutions.

In the context of Microsoft technology, this means AI tools like Copilot and Azure AI must be used within clear governance frameworks to prevent misuse or unintended outcomes. Microsoft's Responsible AI principles emphasize transparency, fairness, privacy, and accountability (`https://www.microsoft.com/en-us/ai/principles-and-approach`). Organizations must ensure these principles are embedded in the design and use of Microsoft AI solutions to fully leverage their potential while managing risk.

This foundation of core principles sets the stage for designing a comprehensive governance framework. By aligning technical practices with human values and clear obligations, organizations can create the scaffolding needed to support responsible, scalable, and adaptive AI systems.

To make these principles actionable, let's discuss how to construct practical governance frameworks, including the roles of different stakeholders, the importance of continuous monitoring, and real-world practices that bring governance to life. This is how we turn principles into action, with specific tools, frameworks, and dialogues to support dynamic governance strategies.

6.3 Designing a Governance Framework

Designing governance for agentic AI requires comprehensive mapping of stakeholders and what aspect of the AI system they own. Think of it like who an intern reports to and, therefore, who's responsible for their behavior and outputs.

This usually includes IT, legal, compliance, business units, and cross-discipline committees. Each of these groups and the diversity of their perspectives plays a crucial role in ensuring AI is used ethically and effectively because with everyone viewing the system from different eyes, the likelihood of awareness blind spots in the initiative are significantly lower.

- IT teams oversee the technical infrastructure, ensuring model reliability and security.
- Legal teams monitor compliance with regulations and assess liability.
- Compliance teams enforce policies and document adherence.
- Business units define the use cases and goals for AI deployments.
- Ethics committees assess fairness, bias, and societal impact.

Each stakeholder's role is distinct yet interconnected, forming a holistic governance structure. Layered controls like human-in-the-loop (HITL) processes, audit trails, and model validation ensure decisions are auditable and aligned with policies. Human-in-the-loop practices involve designated decision-makers reviewing and approving actions suggested by AI agents, while audit logs provide traceability for decisions and allow organizations to detect and correct errors.

Some areas of Microsoft's AI Stack come with these HITL capabilities built in. For example, when using a custom GPT in a Power Automate flow, the flow will, by default, request a human approval action to be added to the flow to approve the AI output before the rest of the flow runs.

Additionally, continuous monitoring, with real-time dashboards and alerts, provides proactive governance and enables immediate response to emerging issues. This approach ensures that governance is dynamic and responsive, not static and reactive, which is critical for maintaining trust and compliance in rapidly evolving AI environments. Microsoft provides telemetry tools within the Power Platform or the Azure AI Foundry Observability dashboard that offers rich monitoring and diagnostic capabilities for AI agents.

These tools enable organizations to collect data on agent performance, identify bottlenecks, track issues, and gain insights into system behavior. Coupled with their adaptive learning capabilities, these telemetry tools support continuous improvement by informing model adjustments, surfacing usage patterns, and flagging anomalies, thereby enabling organizations to evolve their AI agents in alignment with governance objectives and user needs.

Will: "Governance isn't a one-time checklist. It's a living system that evolves as models adapt and business needs shift."

Nancie: "That's why it's so important to have cross-functional conversations about governance. IT, legal, business units, ethics teams, they all need to talk to each other. Governance isn't a siloed task."

Will: "It's a balancing act of keeping things in control while not bogging them down. And those conversations are what make governance frameworks effective in real-world scenarios."

Nancie: "Plus, involving multiple perspectives helps us catch blind spots we might otherwise miss. That's essential when AI is making decisions that affect customers and employees."

But insight alone won't stop a misconfigured agent in its tracks. You need concrete, scenario-driven playbooks that translate monitoring signals into action, before a small anomaly becomes a major incident.

6.4 Building Governance Playbooks

Playbooks provide the actionable steps your teams follow when AI risk indicators surface. They combine

1. **Decision trees and escalation paths:** Who gets alerted when a bias check fails or a drift threshold is crossed?

2. **Scenario protocols**: Step-by-step guides for common issues: model drift, data poisoning, permission errors, or compliance triggers.

3. **Roles and responsibilities**: Clear ownership for every decision, from the first alert to remediation.

A "Bias and Safety Pipeline"

Embed bias and safety checks into both pre-deployment and runtime stages:

- **Pre-deployment**
  - Rigorous testing and red-teaming (attacking your own AI system to identify and address vulnerabilities) before any agent goes live
  - Ethical guidelines review (data sources, label definitions, policy validation)
  - Stakeholder sign-off and compliance hooks
- **Runtime**
  - Continuous learning loops that retrain models on flagged edge-cases
  - Real-time transparency logs and override controls ("kill-switch")
  - Automated drift alerts with human-in-the-loop validation

Don't forget the data layer. For teams using Microsoft Fabric, OneLake data domains, Purview sensitivity labels, and Fabric's row-level security let you lock down which tables an agent can query and potentially log every read/write back to Sentinel for forensic review. Fabric Activator can raise an alert the moment a query returns out-of-policy results, piping that signal straight into your runtime playbook. By embedding these Fabric guard-rails into the same pipeline, security and data governance become first-class citizens alongside bias, drift, and model health.

Here's how that looks in practice:

Imagine a bank deploys an autonomous loan-approval agent on Azure AI Foundry. Before launch, the testing team runs adversarial synthetic-applicant tests to uncover potential race bias. They spot two ZIP-code-based features that act as race proxies and remove them. An ethics review confirms minimal disparity across protected groups, and leadership signs off.

After go-live, telemetry detects a sudden approval-rate drift for Hispanic applicants. The playbook triggers automatically: traffic rolls back to the previous model version, and both the data scientist and governance officer are paged. Within hours the data scientist runs a drift-analysis notebook, the governance officer convenes a root-cause huddle, and legal drafts any required disclosures. The team then re-weights the offending features, retrains, and updates the playbook, turning a potential compliance crisis into a swift, safe remediation that reassures customers and regulators alike.

Nancie: "A playbook is like an emergency plan. It's not just about having one; it's about rehearsing it and refining it based on what you learn."

Will: "And it's not just about preparing for the obvious problems. We need to simulate the weird, the unexpected, the crisis scenarios. That's where playbooks really prove their worth."

Nancie: "And the more we involve people from different roles in these rehearsals, the better prepared we'll be. Cross-team collaboration is essential."

Will: "It's like fire drills for your AI systems. You hope you never need to use them, but if you do, everyone needs to know what to do and when."

Microsoft provides extensive resources for AI risk mitigation that can inform governance playbooks. Their "Guide for Securing the AI-Powered Enterprise" outlines phased approaches to security, governance, and cross-team collaboration (`https://www.microsoft.com/en-us/microsoft-cloud/blog/2025/04/23/securing-ai-navigating-risks-and-compliance-for-the-future`). The "Taxonomy of Failure Modes in Agentic AI Systems" by Microsoft's AI Red Team categorizes risks such as memory poisoning and agent compromise, offering mitigation strategies (`https://www.microsoft.com/en-us/security/blog/2025/04/24/new-whitepaper-outlines-the-taxonomy-of-failure-modes-in-ai-agents`). Microsoft's "Overreliance on AI" framework emphasizes human oversight and critical assessment of AI outputs (`https://learn.microsoft.com/en-us/ai/playbook/technology-guidance/overreliance-on-ai/overreliance-on-ai`). Security tools like Microsoft Defender and Purview, along with the Copilot Control System, offer comprehensive support for data access governance, threat protection, and performance tracking (`https://www.microsoft.com/en-us/security/blog/2025/05/19/microsoft-extends-zero-trust-to-secure-the-agentic-workforce`) (`https://news.microsoft.com/source/features/ai/ai-agents-what-they-are-and-how-theyll-change-the-way-we-work`).

Risk Checklist:

- **Unclear Roles and Escalation Paths:** Can delay response and worsen incidents.

- **Incomplete Scenario Coverage:** May leave teams unprepared for unexpected challenges.

- **Outdated Documentation:** Leads to confusion and inefficiency during crises.

- **Insufficient Training:** Results in poor decisions under pressure.

- **Lack of Continuous Refinement:** Causes governance gaps to widen over time.
- **No Practice Simulations:** Reduces preparedness and resilience.

As we move from building governance playbooks to addressing broader governance challenges, it's clear that playbooks alone aren't enough. Organizations must anticipate the pitfalls and complexities that arise as agentic AI systems scale.

6.5 Challenges and Pitfalls

If governance becomes overly restrictive, it can stifle innovation. Conversely, too little oversight exposes organizations to risk. Like the Goldilocks story, finding the right balance is essential, neither too rigid to halt innovation nor too lenient to invite risk. Misalignment between AI governance and agile development creates gaps. Organizations must avoid treating governance as a checkbox exercise.

Will: "The challenge is balancing agility with control. Too many rules, and you slow down. Too few, and you risk chaos."

Nancie: "It's like trying to steer a ship through rough waters. Too rigid, and you can't respond to waves. Too loose, and you'll drift off course."

Will: "And sometimes the waves are regulations, market demands, or even unexpected AI behavior. We need governance frameworks that help us adjust the sails, not just drop anchor."

Nancie: "I like that. Governance isn't about slowing down, it's about staying on course while adapting to change."

With those waves in mind, it helps to look at how this balance plays out in different environments because "just right" governance looks very different depending on the industry and use case.

For example, in a highly regulated industry like financial services, stringent governance is essential to manage compliance with complex regulations, but overregulation can make it difficult for teams to innovate or adapt to changes in market conditions. By contrast, in a manufacturing context, the focus of AI governance may lean more toward ensuring operational efficiency and safety. Here, the key challenge is balancing AI autonomy with the need for human oversight on the shop floor.

Taken together, these scenarios make one point clear: effective AI governance isn't one-size-fits-all; it must flex to the realities of each sector, striking a balance between stability and agility. Organizations that lean too hard on rules can suffocate innovation and frustrate employees, while those with minimal oversight invite catastrophic failures from data breaches to flawed decision-making. The task is to calibrate guardrails to the level of autonomy, business stakes, and regulatory pressure in your circumstance.

Furthermore, emerging risks like adversarial attacks, AI drift, and compliance gaps must be proactively identified and mitigated. Governance must strike a balance between stability and adaptability, ensuring that guardrails are in place while allowing room for innovation and agility. This approach not only safeguards the organization but also empowers teams to experiment with AI capabilities responsibly.

6.6 From Compliance to Competitive Edge

Most teams treat governance as a brake pedal; something that slows them down just enough to avoid regulatory collisions. In practice, a well-designed responsible-AI framework is more like traction control: it keeps the wheels gripping the road and lets you accelerate faster than competitors who are still spinning in uncertainty.

Trust can be a hidden profit center. An Accenture study found that companies deploying "trustworthy AI" captured up to an 18% revenue lift over peers because customers and employees were more willing to use, recommend, and pay for systems whose decisions they could understand and contest.[1] When a loan applicant sees a plain-language rationale, credit-score threshold, income-to-debt ratio, verifiable employment, approval feels intuitive rather than arbitrary. That single moment of clarity cements loyalty more effectively than any marketing campaign.

Will: "So governance isn't just a seatbelt; it can also be a sales engine."

Nancie: "Confidence converts. If users believe the agent is fair and explainable, they'll lean on it more and tell others to do the same."

---

[1] **Accenture,** *Responsible AI: From Risk Mitigation to Value Creation,* **2023.** https://www.accenture.com/content/dam/accenture/final/accenture-com/document-3/Accenture-Responsible-AI-From-Risk-Mitigation-to-Value-Creation.pdf

Four ways responsible AI drives upside:

Governance pillar	Business benefit
Explainability (transparent logic and model cards)	Shorter sales cycles: enterprise buyers clear procurement hurdles faster when they can audit decision paths.
Traceability (versioned data lineage and audit logs)	Lower support costs: ops teams resolve disputes in minutes, not days, by replaying agent decisions.
Fairness and bias testing	Market expansion: inclusive models approve or recommend previously underserved segments, unlocking new revenue.
Privacy-by-design and security	Partnership magnet: regulated ecosystems (banks, hospitals, governments) prefer vendors that can prove zero-trust controls and safe data handling.

Look to inspire, not just insure.

Begin by *narrating the why*: whenever an agent renders a decision, surface a plain-language rationale—"Approved because the income-to-debt ratio is under 30% and the credit score exceeds 680." That single sentence turns opaque math into conversation and instantly raises user engagement. Next, *teach the user* by embedding a "Why did I get this?" link or hover card that unpacks the key features, data sources, and confidence range behind the outcome; doing so dissolves the lingering "AI is magic" myth. Then *close the loop*: invite customers to challenge or correct results, and feed those corrections straight into the continuous-learning pipeline—proof that the system values human agency rather than replacing it. Finally, *show, don't tell*: live dashboards that track fairness metrics, error rates, and model drift reassure executives and auditors alike that governance is active, not ornamental, converting compliance artifacts into everyday confidence signals.

Will: *"Funny thing we started building guardrails so regulators wouldn't fine us. Turns out they doubled as handrails that help customers climb aboard."*

Nancie: *"And the higher the trust, the steeper the growth curve."*

In short, governance done right is a growth strategy. It reduces downside risk *and* unlocks upside value by turning compliance artifacts into confidence signals. Now, let's go beyond playbooks to the regulatory landscape, how evolving global regulations and adaptive governance agents will keep raising the bar for both protection and performance.

6.7 The Future of AI Governance

Your governance roadmap should look to lean on adaptive systems that can self-monitor and self-correct. Regulatory changes, such as global AI compliance standards, will necessitate agile governance strategies. Embedding governance into AI design, from explainable algorithms to fairness-aware models, will shift governance from reactive to proactive.

Different regions are setting their own pace, focus, and price tag for non-compliance.

Under the newly agreed EU AI Act, a company that deploys a prohibited practice (for example, emotion recognition in schools) can be fined up to €35 million or 7% of its worldwide turnover—whichever is higher; lesser breaches still carry penalties of €15 million/3% or €7.5 million/1% for documentation errors. Because enforcement is delegated to each member state, a pan-European rollout gone wrong could expose a firm to that sanction in every country where the violation occurs (artificialintelligenceact.eu, Holistic AI, Reuters).

Canada's draft **Artificial Intelligence and Data Act (Bill C-27)** proposes administrative monetary penalties that can reach **C$10 million or 3% of global revenue per contravention**, on top of potential Criminal Code liability for reckless deployment of "high-impact" systems (ISED Canada).

Singapore's *Model AI Governance Framework* relies more on certification and reputational levers, while Japan's 2025 **AI Promotion Act** currently imposes *no monetary fines*, betting instead on transparency and government "guidance" notices (PDPC, Future of Privacy Forum).

These geographical differences illustrate the need for organizations to ground their governance frameworks with local expectations and legal mandates. Organizations should also consider how geopolitical shifts and emerging markets will influence regulatory landscapes, adapting their governance strategies to maintain compliance and competitive advantage.

A euro-zone retailer, for instance, may cap the automated-decision scope of its customer-service agent to "low-risk" tasks until a full EU-AI-Act conformity assessment is complete. A Canadian bank might build kill-switches that default to human review whenever a lending model steps outside its audited data domain because each unlogged decision could, in theory, be a million-dollar mistake.

Beyond geography, industry-specific dynamics also play a pivotal role in shaping governance strategies. For instance, in healthcare, AI governance must account for patient safety, data privacy, and regulatory compliance like HIPAA in the United

States or GDPR in Europe. In retail, the emphasis is on consumer data protection and personalization algorithms, while in manufacturing, focus lies on safety protocols and operational efficiencies. Financial services demand stringent controls for fraud detection, risk management, and regulatory reporting. Each industry requires tailored governance frameworks that reflect its unique operational context and regulatory requirements, ensuring responsible and effective use of agentic AI systems.

Nancie: "Imagine governance agents watching the AI agents ensuring alignment, compliance, and continuous learning. That's where we're headed."

Will: "It's not just about compliance anymore it's about resilience and adaptability in real time. Imagine a future where governance adapts dynamically, almost like having a digital immune system for your AI."

Nancie: "And with evolving regional and industry regulations, we'll need frameworks that can flex without breaking. Governance can't be static in a world where everything is accelerating."

Will: "That's the challenge and the opportunity. Dynamic governance lets organizations scale AI without losing sight of trust, ethics, and human-centered design."

Leadership Checklist: Responsible Agentic AI Readiness

✓ **Adopt Core Principles**

- **Implement the seven pillars**: Transparency, Fairness, Accountability, Human Oversight, Privacy and Security, Data Integrity, Clear Objectives
- Tie each to measurable KPIs

✓ **Define Roles and Responsibilities**

- Create a clear RACI map for data, models, overrides, and compliance.
- Review ownership quarterly.

✓ **Build a Bias and Safety Pipeline**

- Require red-teaming and adversarial testing before deployment.
- Enforce model cards, ethics sign-off, and drift-alert thresholds.

✓ Create and Rehearse Playbooks

- Document decision trees and escalation paths.
- Run at least two "AI fire drills" per year and update playbooks after tests or incidents.

✓ Enable Monitoring and Telemetry

- Activate Azure AI Foundry or Power Platform observability for all agents.
- Track fairness metrics, latency, and kill-switch activations.

✓ Stay Ahead of Regulations

- Map your operating regions to local laws (EU AI Act, Bill C-27, etc.).
- Assign compliance stewards for each region.

✓ Embed Industry-Specific Controls

- Integrate standards like HIPAA, PCI, or ISO into workflows.
- Validate via internal or third-party audits.

✓ Turn Trust into a Growth Lever

- Add "Why did I get this?" rationales to user interfaces.
- Measure NPS and conversion lift from explainable outputs.

✓ Invest in Culture and Upskilling

- Train teams quarterly on responsible-AI practices.
- Tie governance KPIs to performance reviews.

✓ Close the Feedback Loop

- Conduct post-incident reviews and update models/playbooks.
- Feed user corrections into retraining cycles.

Agentic AI's potential is immense, but so are the stakes. Robust governance rooted in transparency, fairness, accountability, and adaptability, will empower organizations to harness AI while safeguarding trust and ethics. With thoughtful design, continuous oversight, and a culture of responsibility, agentic AI can be a catalyst for transformative innovation.

Will: "We've built the guardrails and watchtowers; governance really is the backbone of safe, agentic AI."

Nancie: "Absolutely. But a frame needs inhabitants. Without the right people, skills, and culture, even the best governance can gather dust."

Cal: "So in Chapter 7, let's put people at the center. We'll show how to cultivate an AI-ready culture, upskill your workforce, and equip leaders to steer this transformation."

Will: "Think of it as moving from 'Can we do this?' to 'Will we do this together?'"

Nancie: "We'll dig into change-management playbooks, learning journeys, and leadership sprints that make adoption stick."

Cal: "Because sustainable success comes when governance meets human grit and that's exactly where we're headed next."

CHAPTER 7

Embracing the Agentic Workforce

You've just returned from a leadership offsite. The executive team is buzzing about the new AI roadmap, and everyone is excited about what agentic AI could mean for the future of your company. But as you walk back into the office, you see skeptical faces. Some employees are worried AI will replace them. Others are confused about how it fits into their workflow. Your inbox is flooded with messages: "Will we be retrained?" "Who owns the outputs of the AI agents?" "How do I make sure the agent doesn't make a mistake on my behalf?" The contrast is stark, boardroom enthusiasm vs. frontline uncertainty. In that moment, it becomes clear: a roadmap is only as strong as your culture, capabilities, and change management strategy.

The promise of agentic AI is transformative, but its success hinges not only on the sophistication of the technology but on the readiness of the people who use it. As organizations experiment with autonomous agents, Copilot capabilities, and evolving workflows, the human dimension becomes the deciding factor. How will teams adapt? Will employees trust and collaborate with their digital colleagues? What does it take to shift from adoption to acceleration? These questions move beyond IT and into the heart of organizational strategy. In this chapter, we explore how leading companies, including Microsoft's Frontier Firms, are navigating this shift by investing in culture, capability-building, and change leadership to empower their workforce for the era of agentic AI.

CHAPTER 7   EMBRACING THE AGENTIC WORKFORCE

7.1 The Human Side of the Agentic Revolution

Agentic AI Falters in Cultures of Fear and Resistance

Nancie: "You know, Will, as we discussed in Chapter 3, I have been thinking about the Industrial Revolutions of the past, and Adam Smith's division of labor. Each wave changed how people worked, not just what they did."

Will: "And now with agentic AI, we're seeing another revolution, digital colleagues who can think, act, and adapt. But adoption isn't just about tech; it's about trust, roles, and culture."

Culture shapes how people engage with new tools. Even the most advanced agentic AI can't succeed in a culture of fear or resistance. Leaders must create psychological safety, encourage experimentation, and clarify how agents fit into the evolving roles of human workers. Microsoft calls the organizations that excel at this: **"Frontier Firms"**; organizations at the forefront of adopting and *scaling* innovative technologies, including AI, to drive business transformation. A Frontier Firm, as defined by Microsoft, is an organization that not only leads in technological adoption but also sets the benchmark for **responsible, high impact use of AI**, positioning itself as an industry leader in digital transformation. These firms embed continuous learning, employee inclusion, and tight feedback loops into their operating model so that AI is always aligned with organizational purpose and people strategies, turning technological advantage into cultural momentum.

Organizations that disallow AI usage altogether risk creating shadow AI: unauthorized or ungoverned use of tools by employees trying to maintain their productivity. This mirrors past lessons from the introduction of the Internet and mobile devices in the workplace. Banning access did not stop adoption; it merely drove it underground. The smarter move is to embrace the tools, set guardrails, and empower people to use them responsibly.

Will: "It reminds me of the early days of mobile phones at work. IT tried to block usage, but people just found workarounds."

Nancie: "And when companies embraced mobile with policies and tools, productivity soared. The same will be true of AI."

To that end, the emotional component of transformation must not be underestimated. Fear of obsolescence, concern about fairness, and confusion about new roles are all valid responses to change. Organizations that take time to listen, using empathy mapping, pulse surveys, or Microsoft Viva insights, will be better positioned to respond.

Will: *"A data analyst recently told me, 'This tool is amazing but it makes me question my future.'"*

Nancie: *"And that's a real sentiment. We must meet it with honesty and purpose. Employees aren't just resources, they're our partners in innovation."*

Agentic AI doesn't need to threaten jobs. In fact, when implemented well, it can restore craftsmanship by taking away the digital noise. It allows employees to do fewer things better, reclaiming depth over breadth.

Nancie: *"Think of it like the move from a generalist craftsman to a specialist artisan, AI gives us the space to be excellent again."*

Will: *"And like Adam Smith said, specialization drives innovation. That hasn't changed."*

Successful AI transformation requires a cultural mindset shift, from controlling processes to guiding outcomes. It also means being honest about what AI can and cannot do. This honesty builds trust. Employees need to see AI as a teammate, not a threat.

Not all organizations are starting from the same cultural baseline when it comes to AI readiness. Just as digital maturity varies widely across industries and firms, so too does cultural readiness for working alongside agentic AI. One helpful framing is to think in terms of a **cultural readiness spectrum**, which moves from *resistant* to *reactive*, *aware*, *engaged*, and finally *adaptive*.

- At the **resistant** end, organizations have low trust in new technologies and high fear of job disruption. AI is viewed as a threat, not a tool. These environments often lack psychological safety and discourage experimentation.

- The **reactive** stage reflects companies that adopt AI out of competitive pressure rather than vision. They may roll out tools hastily without investing in employee engagement or understanding. Missteps are common here due to lack of shared purpose.

- **Awareness** is a turning point. Organizations begin to understand that success depends on people as much as tools. Training programs and town halls emerge, but they may still be inconsistent or opt-in only.

- **Engaged** cultures begin to shift the mindset. Employees participate in co-creating AI workflows, feedback loops are strong, and experimentation is encouraged. Leaders model AI use and storytelling helps demystify the technology.

- At the **adaptive** end, AI becomes a cultural muscle. Teams are empowered, governance is collaborative, and learning is continuous. These organizations treat change as a constant and are ready to evolve roles and processes as AI capabilities advance.

Beyond adaptive, companies that are of the "AI-First," Frontier Firm belief structure are operating with a culture of continuous reinvention. This is where the organization "blends machine intelligence with human judgment," scales AI across business units, and deeply installs continuous-learning loops, RAI governance, and an AI-centered belief system into its operating model.

Understanding where your culture sits on this spectrum can help tailor change strategies. Moving forward doesn't require perfection, it requires awareness and intentional steps toward a more open, inclusive, and agentic-ready culture.

7.2 Building AI Fluency and Capabilities That Scale

Rolling out agentic AI isn't a training exercise, it's a capability evolution.

Will: *"Nancie, remember when you first introduced CRM systems in the 1990s? The hardest part wasn't the tech, it was helping people understand how to use it well enough to actually change how they worked. It has long been about adoption."*

Nancie: *"And now with agentic AI, we're asking people not just to adopt a tool but to delegate thinking and decision-making to it. That's a whole new level of capability development."*

Rolling out agentic AI successfully requires more than training sessions or lunch-and-learns. It demands a shift in organizational capability, what people know, what they can do, and how they adapt. Microsoft's *Frontier Firm* research underscores this point: leading organizations invest in skills at every level of the business, not just in technical roles. They understand that scaling AI use depends on everyone from the service desk to the C-suite being able to recognize where and how AI agents can be used to enhance value.

This starts with digital literacy and grows into AI fluency. Employees must be empowered to ask the right questions of their agents, interpret outputs critically, and know when to override or escalate decisions. This requires both individual learning and team-based capability building. It also requires leaders to model the behavior, showcasing how they themselves are working with agents to save time, generate insights, or automate decision cycles.

To support this evolution, organizations should

- Create internal capability academies focused on prompt engineering, ethical AI usage, and agent supervision.

- Use role-based simulations to help employees learn by doing in a risk-free setting; Think **"promptathons"**—rapid-fire workshops where teams draft, test, and refine prompts together, sharing insights in real time.

- Offer just-in-time learning tools and embedded nudges within the software (like Copilot tips and Microsoft Viva modules).

Moreover, capability development must be ongoing. The rapid evolution of agentic AI tools means yesterday's best practice can become today's risk. A continuous learning strategy, supported by platforms like Microsoft Learn and LinkedIn Learning, ensures employees remain confident and competent.

Will: *"It's funny, AI agents aren't just changing workflows, they're changing what it means to be capable. It's not about memorizing procedures anymore, it's about learning how to collaborate with intelligence."*

Nancie: *"And leaders need to recognize that too. We need to redefine performance metrics and KPIs to reflect how effectively people are leveraging AI. Otherwise, we'll end up rewarding the skills of the past."*

Digital fluency is no longer optional. Agentic AI demands a workforce that understands not just how to use AI but how to question, supervise, and co-create with it. Microsoft's Frontier Firm research notes that 78% of leaders in AI-forward companies are investing in role-specific AI training, not generic upskilling (https://www.microsoft.com/en-us/worklab/frontier).

Shopify offers a glimpse of how this expectation is hardening into policy: in an April 2025 internal memo that quickly went viral, CEO Tobi Lütke made AI competence a baseline condition for career growth. Every employee must run an "AI special project," AI utilization will be scored in performance reviews, and no new headcount will be approved until teams prove that autonomous agents can't do the job first (theverge.com).

The message from both Microsoft's data and Shopify's mandate is clear: **AI fluency is becoming a promotion criterion and a gating factor for resources,** an essential capability, not a nice-to-have.

Will: "It's not about turning everyone into a data scientist. It's about helping people ask better questions, judge AI outputs, and feel confident that they can steer their digital teammates."

Nancie: "I've seen this firsthand. When employees understand how the AI agent works, they're more likely to use it responsibly and more creatively."

Effective fluency programs include use-case simulations, scenario planning, prompt writing workshops, and peer learning. Frontier Firms are also embedding Copilot skills into onboarding, performance reviews, and leadership development, ensuring that AI isn't seen as a bolt-on but as a core capability.

7.3 Evolving the Employee Experience

Rolling out agentic AI isn't a tech deployment, it's an organizational transformation. That means change management must go deeper than training. Communication, co-design, and co-ownership are critical. Microsoft's Frontier Firm leaders use iterative design processes, often piloting agentic AI in cross-functional teams where frontline workers provide feedback that shapes refinement.

Nancie: "We once ran a pilot where service reps helped train the AI agent. They didn't just accept it, they improved it. That changed everything."

Will: "That's the magic of participatory design. People support what they help create."

Successful change strategies also involve agent stewardship. Leaders must appoint champions who monitor usage, gather feedback, and evolve practices. Microsoft's approach includes AI Change Agents, selected leaders trained to guide AI adoption through their networks, fostering trust and creating a culture of learning and ownership (https://www.microsoft.com/en-us/worklab/frontier).

Agentic AI doesn't replace people, it lets them reclaim the best parts of their jobs

Agentic AI isn't just reshaping tasks, it's reshaping how employees experience their jobs. By offloading repetitive or low-value activities, AI allows workers to focus on more meaningful, strategic, and human-centric aspects of their roles. This shift has profound implications for job satisfaction, engagement, and retention.

From frontline customer service to back-office operations, AI can alleviate common sources of burnout. Copilot features in tools like Microsoft Dynamics 365 and Microsoft 365 enable employees to reduce time spent drafting content, searching for information, or switching between apps. This lowers cognitive load and preserves energy for tasks that require judgment, empathy, or collaboration.

Will: *"When I talk to service agents, they're not afraid of the AI. They're relieved it's taking over the stuff that drains them, like typing case notes or routing tickets."*

Nancie: *"And it's not just service roles. Engineers, marketers, even finance teams are saying they finally have time to think again, to get ahead of the work instead of reacting all the time. They actually get to make a dent in their to-do lists."*

Companies piloting agentic AI are also using it to reimagine job design. Instead of layering more responsibilities onto already stretched workers, they're redistributing tasks in partnership with digital agents. Some organizations are even standing up new specialist roles, from **"AI Experience Managers,"** like the post NatWest created to steward its Cora Copilot program, to **"AI/Agent-Orchestration Leads"** and **"Lead Engineers – AI Agent Orchestration Frameworks"** now appearing across tech job boards and thought-leadership pieces. These hires sit between humans and agents, tuning prompts, overseeing ethics, and measuring adoption so that autonomous systems *enhance* (rather than hinder) day-to-day employee experience (CreativeAIdjinni. coCreativeAIHIJOBSGlassdoordjinni.cobusinessinsider.comdeloitte.com).

When done well, AI implementation becomes a retention strategy. Employees feel supported, empowered, and less overwhelmed. But when done poorly, or imposed or forbidden without context, it can backfire, reinforcing fears of obsolescence or surveillance. That's why transparency, feedback loops, and co-design are critical. The best AI transformations happen *with* employees, not *to* them.

Will: *"It's like we're finally addressing the root cause of disengagement, too much busywork, not enough purpose."*

Nancie: *"Yes and in a tight talent market, that matters more than ever."*

7.4 Change Management for Agentic Transformation

AI doesn't fail because the tech is bad, it fails because change isn't managed.

Nancie: *"Will, you've seen it too, so many AI initiatives stall not from a lack of innovation, but from a lack of change leadership."*

Will: *"Absolutely. Change is always emotional and with AI the emotion is dialed up. Employees are bombarded with headlines about 'job-stealing robots' and viral LinkedIn or TikTok hot-takes that offer only half the story. If we don't frame the why internally, those outside narratives will fill the gap, and people will resist the how before we've even begun."*

Successful adoption of agentic AI requires more than a rollout plan, it demands a strategic change management framework that bridges vision with execution, and aligns leadership with frontline realities. At the heart of this effort is helping people not only understand the shift, but believe in it.

Organizations must anticipate resistance, design for transparency, and create a two-way dialogue from the outset. Some of the most effective programs aim to

- **Identify change champions** across departments who model agentic workflows and mentor peers.
- **Leverage storytelling** to communicate the purpose behind AI initiatives, using real scenarios.
- **Use tools like Microsoft Viva Engage** and **Change Analytics** to track sentiment and adapt messaging.

Many leaders are now applying **Prosci's ADKAR model**, (i.e., Awareness, Desire, Knowledge, Ability, Reinforcement), as a structured way to guide people through AI transformation. Microsoft partners also often use the **Success by Design** framework when deploying AI within Dynamics 365 environments to align governance, training, and change from day one.

Will: *"I spoke with a team where they paired each new agent with a person assigned to be its 'sponsor.' That created ownership and accountability."*

Nancie: *"That's smart. People don't resist change, they resist change they don't understand or feel part of. Make them stakeholders, not bystanders."*

In addition, it's crucial to reframe what success looks like. Early wins shouldn't just be about efficiency metrics, they should include employee confidence, quality of decision-making, and perceived support. Organizations should also **normalize experimentation**, allowing teams to test AI workflows and provide feedback before wide-scale implementation.

By treating agentic AI as a strategic transformation, not just a software upgrade, companies create the conditions for meaningful, lasting change.

7.5 Leadership for the Age of Agents

Leadership is the real differentiator between AI success and shelfware

Traditional leadership emphasizes control and predictability. But agentic AI introduces complexity, unpredictability, and speed. Leaders must shift from directing to orchestrating, from knowing all the answers to asking the right questions.

Will: "*Frontier Firm leaders see themselves less as commanders and more as curators, creating environments where AI agents and humans can thrive together.*"

Nancie: "*And they role model learning. When leaders show curiosity, admit they're still learning, and use AI themselves, it signals that growth is a shared journey.*"

Leadership sets the tone for AI adoption. Champions must communicate a compelling vision and model the behaviors they want to see. When executives use AI tools themselves and share real results, they demystify the technology. Leaders should also

- Embed AI into strategic planning and goal setting.
- Sponsor AI champions across departments.
- Reinforce a growth mindset culture.
- Create accountability for adoption outcomes.

Nancie: "*When leaders show curiosity and vulnerability, 'I'm learning this too,' it gives everyone else permission to do the same.*"

Will: "*Right. It's not about having all the answers. It's about showing that AI is important enough to explore together.*"

Internally at Microsoft, this isn't lip service—it's baked into executive development. As Satya Nadella has observed, "The most successful companies will be those that build AI into the core of their business while aligning leadership and culture around it" (view.email-hmgstrategy.com). Beginning in 2019, Microsoft launched the **AI Business School** to help senior leaders architect AI strategy, culture, and responsibility—not merely to greenlight pilots but to become outspoken champions of AI-driven transformation (The Official Microsoft Blog). In April 2025, the **Inside Track** blog detailed how Microsoft Digital united **Viva Learning** and **Microsoft Learn** into a comprehensive AI curriculum—"not just winning with technology—it's about supporting the community and doing things the right way" (Microsoft). Most recently, the **Microsoft 365 Copilot Blog** published *Rewriting the IT Playbook,* framing its executive playbook around three pillars—leadership, human change, and technical readiness—explicitly guiding CIOs to shift from merely approving AI to actively advocating and embedding it in culture and governance from Day One (techcommunity.microsoft.com).

Thinking through different leadership archetypes will help this change journey, each part of your organization will have different *leadership personas* for navigating AI transformation:

- **The Visionary:** Focused on strategic outcomes and aligning AI efforts with business value.
- **The Coach:** Empowers teams to experiment, learn, and build AI fluency.
- **The Skeptic:** Cautious but necessary to ask hard questions about ethics, risk, and value.
- **The Collaborator:** Breaks down silos and fosters cross-functional alignment between AI, IT, business, and people teams.

It's not a road without its bumps, there are some *common leadership missteps* when introducing AI:

- Delegating AI responsibility solely to IT.
- Failing to model AI use personally.
- Over-indexing on efficiency metrics at the expense of trust.
- Not investing in communication and storytelling.

Will: "Nancie, rumor has it you sparked an AI craze in your practice with, of all things, a vacuum-cleaner purchase. How did that become a teaching moment?"

Nancie (laughing): "I was paralyzed by a thousand models online, so I asked ChatGPT to shortlist three based on price, noise level, and pet hair. Five minutes later I had my pick, and a light-bulb moment. In our next team huddle I told that story and set a challenge:

'This week, use Copilot or ChatGPT on **one** everyday task anything from drafting an email to planning dinner. Then share what you learned.' The point wasn't the appliance, it was proving how quickly AI can shave hours off the mundane."

Will: "So the message wasn't 'become prompt engineers overnight,' it was 'start small, get comfortable, then scale the wins.' How did the team respond?"

Nancie: "Practice meetings can now include mini show-and-tells. A consultant cut proposal formatting time in half; a PM used Copilot to summarize a 40-page SOW. Once people felt a personal benefit, they were eager to apply AI to client work. That single anecdote kicked off a culture of low-risk experimentation."

Will: "Perfect illustration of the **Coach** archetype, empowering teams to try, learn, and share."

When leaders model curiosity and make AI approachable, they lower the psychological barrier for everyone else. The lesson: you don't need a moon-shot to start; a vacuum cleaner (or any everyday task) will do. What matters is turning those micro-wins into a habit of continuous improvement, then embedding that habit in formal programs like Microsoft's "AI for Leaders," where technical literacy meets change-leadership practice.

7.6 Aligning Organizational Design to Support AI

Organizational structures need to evolve to support distributed intelligence. This may mean new roles like AI ethicists, prompt engineers, or agentic process designers. Frontier Firms are also creating AI Centers of Excellence to govern tools, templates, and training centrally, while empowering business units to localize adoption (https://www.microsoft.com/en-us/worklab/frontier).

Will: "Think of it as moving from a pyramid to a network. Intelligence doesn't live at the top anymore, it's embedded everywhere."

Nancie: "And that's why roles need redefining. The org chart should reflect collaboration between people and AI agents, not just departments."

Governance, reporting lines, and incentive structures must adapt. For instance, performance metrics may now include how effectively employees leverage agents, or how responsibly they train and supervise them.

Resistance is natural. AI challenges deeply held beliefs about value, control, and competence. To address this, organizations need empathy-driven strategies. This includes

- Transparent communication about AI's purpose and limitations
- Townhalls/community discussions and feedback sessions
- Creating roles like AI Coaches or Digital Change Agents

Will: *"Trust doesn't come from a launch email. It comes from consistent, respectful engagement."*

Nancie: *"People need to feel heard and supported, not just 'trained.' That's how you win hearts and minds."*

Trust is especially critical in sectors like healthcare and government, where decisions carry significant personal or societal weight. Remember, Responsible AI practices, including bias checks and human-in-the-loop protocols, must be explained in human terms, not just technical ones.

Additionally, fostering cross-functional collaboration is crucial for AI adoption. This involves creating cross-disciplinary teams that include technical experts, business leaders, and ethical thinkers. These teams can collaborate on AI projects to ensure they are practical, innovative, and ethically sound. While centralized AI Centers of Excellence (CoEs) govern AI tools and templates, business units should have the autonomy to localize adoption based on specific departmental needs.

A dynamic governance framework is necessary to manage AI adoption. This includes creating agile processes for data usage, algorithm transparency, and real-time feedback to improve AI models. Data governance is particularly important to ensure the quality, fairness, and ethical use of data in AI training. Moreover, organizations must establish AI ethics committees and ensure regular audits to mitigate biases and ensure accountability in AI-driven decisions.

To create a culture of AI-driven innovation, organizations should encourage experimentation, reward innovative AI applications, and incentivize employees to think creatively about AI's potential. At the same time, AI security and privacy must be a top priority, with organizations investing in cybersecurity measures and ensuring compliance with data protection regulations.

Finally, scaling AI adoption requires robust IT infrastructure that can accommodate growing AI needs, such as cloud resources and data storage. AI tools must be seamlessly integrated into existing business systems, such as CRM and ERP platforms, to optimize workflows and improve data-driven decision-making. Partnerships with AI startups, research institutions, and other organizations can further support AI adoption, ensuring access to cutting-edge technologies and collaborative projects that enhance AI capabilities.

7.7 Scaling Sustainably

Scaling agentic AI isn't about adding more tools, it's about adding more value. That means focusing on sustainable adoption. Microsoft emphasizes responsible scaling practices, ensuring agents are deployed where they add measurable benefit, aligned with clear governance.

Frontier Firms track agent impact through metrics like task acceleration, employee satisfaction, and outcome quality. They use Microsoft's Power Platform telemetry to monitor agent usage, surface anomalies, and identify opportunities to evolve prompts and workflows (https://www.microsoft.com/en-us/worklab/frontier).

Nancie: "Scaling is a discipline. If you don't have monitoring, feedback loops, and alignment, more AI agents just means more confusion."

Will: "Yes, and more technical debt. Scale what works, sunset what doesn't, and constantly refine. That's the difference between AI that delivers and AI that drifts."

Scaling agentic AI is about ensuring that AI creates tangible, long-term value. Sustainable adoption is key, meaning organizations should prioritize strategies that allow AI tools to integrate deeply into existing workflows and processes, rather than using AI as a one-off solution. This requires organizations to focus on responsible scaling practices, where AI agents are deployed in areas that can demonstrate measurable benefits. It's not just about increasing the number of tasks automated; it's about enhancing the quality, efficiency, and relevance of AI implementations in business functions. AI adoption must be aligned with a clear governance framework to ensure transparency, accountability, and ethical usage across the organization.

To successfully scale agentic AI, companies need to track and measure the impact of AI deployments. This involves developing metrics that go beyond basic output and delve into key performance indicators such as task acceleration, employee satisfaction, and overall outcome quality. These metrics not only help determine the efficiency of AI agents but also gauge their effectiveness in enhancing the user experience. Frontier Firms, for example, track the impact of their AI deployments by measuring these variables. Through tools like Microsoft's Power Platform telemetry, these firms can monitor AI agent usage in real time, surfacing anomalies or issues that may arise and identifying areas where improvements can be made.

Telemetry data from the Power Platform can be used to continuously refine AI implementations. By analyzing how agents interact with users and identifying patterns in their performance, businesses can evolve prompts, adjust workflows, and optimize AI tools to better meet the needs of their teams. This iterative approach ensures that AI adoption isn't a static process but a dynamic one, allowing organizations to adapt and enhance their AI capabilities as their needs evolve. By continuously refining AI systems based on real-world data, organizations can ensure that AI becomes a sustainable, high-impact tool that drives consistent value across the business, making it a strategic asset for the long term.

Leader's Checklist: Equipping the Agentic Workforce

- ☑ Foster a culture of trust, experimentation, and psychological safety around AI use.
- ☑ Acknowledge and address employee fears about AI replacement early and openly.
- ☑ Establish clear governance to prevent shadow AI use and encourage responsible adoption.
- ☑ Build role-specific AI fluency through ongoing training and simulations.
- ☑ Update KPIs to reflect AI collaboration, not just individual output.
- ☑ Redesign roles and workflows to align with human-agent partnerships.
- ☑ Co-create AI experiences with employees to boost engagement and reduce resistance.
- ☑ Use feedback loops to refine how AI is introduced and supported across the organization.
- ☑ Benchmark progress with peers and learn from Microsoft's *Frontier Firms* research.

CHAPTER 7   EMBRACING THE AGENTIC WORKFORCE

The team gathers around the whiteboard, the "Agentic-Ready" checklist complete. Sunlight filters through the glass walls as Will, Nancie, and Cal reflect on their progress.

Nancie (smiling): "We've nailed data estate, governance, workforce upskilling, and responsible AI practices. Our runway is clear."

Will (nodding): "Chapter 7 laid every plank of the runway—culture, capability, change leadership. Now we're about to take off."

Cal (avatar flickering to life): "Readiness coefficient: 0.93. Recommended next phase: real-world mission profiles to validate operational performance."

Nancie: "Exactly. It's one thing to prepare; it's another to prove it in action. We need to show how these principles play out in our day-to-day lives."

Will: "Then let's bring it to life. In Chapter 8, we follow a senior rep at TeleComX as AI shifts from theory to strategic partner—anticipating needs, guiding decisions, and rewriting what it means to sell."

Cal: "Shall I cue the TeleComX narrative? Beginning with Monday morning pipeline analysis and a Copilot that already knows the customer?"

Nancie (energetic): "Do it. Time to plot the route beyond the horizon."

CHAPTER 8

Beyond the Horizon

It's a busy Monday morning, and as I sip my coffee, I'm already looking at a jam-packed schedule for the day. As a senior sales rep at TeleComX, my mornings are usually filled with back-to-back meetings, follow-up calls, and the constant push to close deals. But today feels a bit different. As I glance at my sales pipeline, one particular lead stands out: a potential corporate client that has been looking for an enterprise-wide broadband solution.

For years, my job has been pretty straightforward: meet with potential clients, assess their needs, and pitch the best solution from our offerings. But lately, things have started changing. I pull up the Copilot app on my tablet, the new AI assistant rolled out across our team, and I see something surprising: Copilot has already analyzed this lead's history, company size, budget, and even previous interactions with customer service. A notification pops up: "Recommended offer: Enterprise plan with custom discounts based on similar industry clients."

I pause. "Okay, that's new," I think to myself. I hadn't even started preparing for the meeting yet, and Copilot is already recommending a solution.

I walk into the conference room, and as I begin my pitch, Copilot seamlessly integrates into the conversation. I don't have to flip through old notes or check systems manually. Copilot pulls up relevant data in real time, showing a detailed breakdown of similar corporate clients who benefitted from the solution. It even predicts potential customer objections based on the client's behavior and suggests tailored counterarguments before they've even been raised.

I continue the conversation, and without missing a beat, Copilot presents me with the next steps. It's like having a strategic partner by my side, anticipating what needs to be said and done. The meeting goes smoothly, and by the time I wrap up, I feel confident that we're moving toward a close.

CHAPTER 8 BEYOND THE HORIZON

After the meeting, I check my tablet, and Copilot has already prepared follow-up emails with personalized offers and next steps, based on the conversation we just had. I don't have to spend hours drafting emails or researching pricing; it's all automated and tailored, right at my fingertips.

As I head to my next meeting, my phone rings. It's Sarah, my manager, giving me an update on something huge. "Rachel, have you seen the latest from our AI team? They've just rolled out an enterprise-wide AI swarm system. The AI is now not just assisting us but also helping predict trends, suggest sales strategies, and even automate follow-ups based on real-time customer interactions. This isn't just about automation, it's about AI actively driving decisions."

I'm amazed. The way AI is now being integrated into the sales process isn't just about saving time; it's about empowering me to be more effective, more strategic, and faster at closing deals.

I finish the call and can't help but reflect on how much my role has already changed. Copilot isn't just an assistant anymore; it's becoming an active participant in my sales strategy. It's not about just fixing problems, it's about enhancing the entire process. I don't spend my days searching for solutions or drafting the perfect pitch anymore. I'm collaborating with a system that anticipates needs, personalizes interactions, and helps me close deals faster and more effectively than ever before.

The future of my work isn't about working harder. It's about working smarter, with AI systems that adapt to every conversation, anticipate every need, and make my work more efficient and impactful.

So far, we've explored

- The gaps in today's AI solutions
- How agency gives AI the ability to fill its own gaps
- How this agentic functionality solves new and existing business problems at a deeper level
- How the mechanics of these solutions manifest in the Microsoft AI Stack
- How to design, develop, and deploy these agentic capabilities in a responsible and trustworthy way
- What this wave of innovation changes for organizations and their workforces

CHAPTER 8   BEYOND THE HORIZON

This was all meant to lay the agentic-ready runway. But once you get there, where can you take things next? What does this evolve into? Is there an endgame?

You've probably heard the expression: "begin with the end in mind" and preparing for/experiencing massive technical renaissance are no different. The clearer you are about the state you'd like to end up in, the clearer the path will be to get there.

As we close out this journey together, we'd like to give you as much of a roadmap as possible for the future trajectories of agentic AI, potential breakthroughs, and emerging research areas that will be important to navigate through as you embrace the agentic AI era.

Nancie (Global CX Lead): *"Alright team, we've ticked every item on the 'agentic-ready' checklist: data estate, governance, workforce upskilling, responsible AI office. That's our runway. The question is: where's the flight plan?"*

Will (Chief AI Architect): *"If Chapters 1-7 built the plane, Chapter 8 plots the route. Think autonomy maturity, pilot-to-fleet scaling, and the regulatory weather ahead."*

Cal (Analytics Agent, avatar flickering to life on the table): *"Telemetry confirms organizational readiness coefficient at **0.87**. Recommended next waypoint sequence:*

1. *Level-Up Autonomy*

2. *Scale into a Fleet*

3. *Harmonize Innovation and Responsibility*

4. *Maximize Human-in-the-Loop*

5. *Adopt AI-First Business Models*

6. *Prepare for the Post-Agent Frontier."*

Nancie (smiling): *"Cal just sketched our chapter outline in six bullet points. But leaders need more than bullets, they need context, stories, and guardrails."*

Will: *"Then let's walk them through each waypoint. We'll show how you evolve from isolated copilots to cross-domain swarms, why a centralized AI fabric matters, and what ethical turbulence to expect."*

Cal: *"Shall I compile real-world benchmarks and emerging research to accompany each section?"*

Nancie: *"Do it. And cue up a closing call-to-action. By the end, readers should know exactly how to chart their own horizon safely and ambitiously."*

Nancie taps the whiteboard. The heading morphs to **8.1 The Autonomy Maturity Path**, and the journey beyond the runway begins.

8.1 The Autonomy Maturity Path

The first wave of AI integration focused largely on task automation, streamlining basic processes, reducing human error, and improving efficiency. But as agentic AI evolves, the next frontier is about building autonomous systems capable of not just performing tasks but independently making decisions and completing processes end-to-end—adapting to new data, evolving to meet new business needs, **and operating within robust guardrails to ensure safe, ethical, and controlled outcomes**.

Organizations are now moving toward creating ecosystems where AI doesn't just **support** human decision-making, but actively **drives** it. These systems, enabled by **self-improving** algorithms and real-time decision-making, will be capable of operating with minimal human intervention, freeing employees to focus on **higher-value tasks**.

Nancie:

*"Will, as **agentic AI** matures, we're heading toward a future where AI not only assists with decisions but also, with trust established, **takes the lead** in many of them. Imagine a scenario where **AI systems** are autonomously managing supply chains or adjusting marketing strategies based on real-time consumer behavior data, without needing constant oversight from human managers."*

Will:

*"Exactly, Nancie. And when AI starts acting more like a **strategic partner**, it's not just about **doing things faster**; it's about doing them with **greater intelligence** and **precision**. It's a huge leap forward from the traditional automation we've seen so far."*

A good way to evaluate your next step on the path is the following ladder:

Maturity tier	Core capability	Human role	Example KPI
Tier 0: Manual + Analytics	Dashboards and rule-based alerts; every action is still point-and-click	Decision-maker performs each step	Time-to-insight = *hours*
Tier 1: Assistive Agents	A single copilot embedded in one tool; executes discrete tasks with a human in the loop	Trigger, review, and validate output	Time-on-task ↓ 20%

(*continued*)

Maturity tier	Core capability	Human role	Example KPI
Tier 2: Coordinated Agents	Goal-seeking, multiagent workflows with shared memory and guardrails; cross-tool orchestration	Set objectives, approve exceptions, escalate edge cases	Throughput ↑ 35% and/or cycle-time ↓ 50%
Tier 3: Swarm Intelligence	Enterprise-wide agent fleet that self-organizes and optimizes across domains	Strategic steering and policy setting	Net-new revenue ↑ 10%

The important things this ladder articulates is that progressing from one tier of autonomy to the next is not simply a technical upgrade. It reshapes risk, data strategy, and organizational design in lockstep. At **Tier 1**, a misconfigured permission might inconvenience a single user; at **Tier 3**, the same lapse could stall an autonomous workflow and invite regulatory scrutiny.

Data that lived happily in departmental silos during pilot projects becomes a liability when agents must reason across finance, supply chain, and customer sentiment in real time. And as decision-rights shift from individual "bot owners" to fleets of collaborating agents, enterprises find themselves formalizing an **AI Command and Control Office** a cross-functional nerve-center that spots drift, resolves conflicts, and aligns machine judgment with business intent.

Let's see how this would work for TeleComX with their potential *Trouble-Ticket Copilot* solution.

Imagine a bright Monday morning at TeleComX. In the bustling Customer Care war room, CSRs lean in as Trouble-Ticket Copilot listens to live call audio, pulls in the latest knowledge-base snippets, and drafts follow-up emails in real time. Each suggestion still lands in a human hand for that final Send click, but the impact is unmistakable: average handle times drop significantly, and customers walk away satisfied more often on the very first call. Here, at Stage 1—Assistive, AI feels like a trusted teammate, always there to lend a hand, never to overstep.

By mid-quarter, the next evolution hums quietly behind the scenes. Two specialized agents, Optimizer and Network Guardian, have taken their posts, sharing telemetry through OneLake and consulting a shared playbook. When a regional router falters, Optimizer springs into action, diagnosing the fault and estimating potential downtime costs. If the forecasted hit tops $10,000, Network Guardian bursts into motion: it issues a vendor-agnostic reset, reroutes traffic, and fires off status updates to customers.

CHAPTER 8   BEYOND THE HORIZON

All of this unfolds before a single human ever opens a dashboard; a neat Teams card presents the entire choreography (diagnosis, repair, notification), for one-click approval. The result? A huge plunge in repair cycle time, and an operations team that now sets objectives and hands off the heavy lifting. This is Stage 2—Coordinated Agents, where multiple AI voices harmonize under clear guardrails.

Fast forward to TeleComX's executive suite, where the true wonder takes shape. A quartet of domain-specialized agents: Guardian for networks, RevenueMaster for pricing, CX Sage for support, and SupplySense for logistics, publishes their evolving goals to a central Swarm Mediator. When CX Sage detects a sudden surge of premium-tier upgrades, it doesn't merely raise a flag; it negotiates extra bandwidth with Guardian, fine-tunes discount campaigns through RevenueMaster, and rebalances spare-parts inventory with SupplySense. All of this transpires in seconds, without a single human ping-ponging between tools. Instead, leadership greets a concise "flight log" each dawn and, with a simple direction: "prioritize margin over growth," steers the entire swarm. At Stage 3—Swarm Intelligence, TeleComX has transformed its countless AI threads into an adaptive, self-optimizing tapestry: the business runs itself, while people chart the course.

Accelerators to Climb the Ladder Faster

Enterprises that sprint up the autonomy curve share four structural boosters:

1. **Unified Data Estate.** By storing embeddings, transactions, and telemetry in a single lake, every agent retrieves the freshest truth without costly context switches.

2. **AgentOps Pipeline.** Continuous integration for prompts, tool definitions, and reward functions means new behaviors ship with the same discipline as modern software releases, and can be rolled back just as cleanly.

3. **Guardrail SDK.** A reusable library of safety checks, audit logs, and escalation routes prevents teams from reinventing governance for every project, accelerating both compliance and innovation.

4. **Skill Marketplace.** Each proven OpenAPI action, be it "adjust invoice" or "reroute shipment," is published once and discoverable by every new agent, letting fresh initiatives start with a toolbox instead of blank code.

Will: "Autonomy licenses are earned like pilot ratings; you log hours, pass the tests, and upgrade your craft."

Nancie: "And leadership supplies the control tower: visibility, governance, and a shared flight plan so every AgentCaptain takes off and lands safely."

8.2 Scaling Agentic AI—From Pilots to Enterprise Flight

Most organizations meet agentic AI in a sandbox: one department stakes a small budget on an experiment, a few enthusiasts nurture it, and the only evidence of success is a handful of happy anecdotes. Breakthrough happens when those isolated victories fuse into a centralized AI fabric, a living utility that every team can draw on, share with, and improve.

In TeleComX's case that fabric would be built on Microsoft Fabric's OneLake. By corralling telemetry, CRM feeds, billing data, and supply-chain events into a single lakehouse, the company eliminates rival "sources of truth." The customer-care agent triaging a drop-call complaint now consults the *same* data the supply-chain optimizer uses to reroute hardware, and both can trust what they see.

The infrastructure does more than tidy data. A unified AgentOps pipeline, essentially MLOps for prompts, tools, and reward functions, pushes every new experiment through the same security scans, rollback hooks, and telemetry dashboards. When HR builds a recruiting bot, it inherits the sentiment-analysis function already battle-tested by Customer Service; when Sales fine-tunes embeddings for churn prediction, Marketing's next campaign benefits without lifting a finger. Value compounds faster than cost, because lessons, code, and guardrails travel on the same rails.

Will: "Think of it as building a single airport hub. Whether you're flying HR, Finance, or Field Service routes, the runways, the control-tower, and the fuel lines are already waiting."

Nancie: "And every new take-off feeds better weather models for the next flight, less turbulence, quicker time-to-value."

Here's an example of what that accelerated journey could look like for TeleComX:

1. **Phase 0: The Department Sandbox**

    Customer Service deploys *Trouble-Ticket Copilot* on a stand-alone SQL replica. It works, but every subsequent pilot must rebuild data pipes and governance artifacts from scratch.

2. **Phase 1: Build the Hub**

   Leadership funds a OneLake AI Fabric. All telemetry, CRM, billing and logistics data lands in one lakehouse; an AgentOps pipeline enforces version control, testing suites, and drift alerts for every prompt and model.

3. **Phase 2: Cross-Pollination**

   The *Sales Searcher* agent reuses the customer-360 table and the sentiment tool blessed by Customer Service; the *Marketing Maven* agent taps the same embeddings to craft hyper-personalized campaigns and streams engagement signals back for Sales scoring.

4. **Phase 3: Fleet Orchestration**

   A *Swarm Mediator* agent now lets domain agents barter data and negotiate priorities. When the *Logistics Scout* agent foresees a shipment delay, it nudges the *CX Sage* agent to warn customers and the *RevenueMaster* agent to adjust refund policy in real time.

5. **Phase 4: Non-linear Lift-Off**

   New business units spin up agents in days rather than months.

   - HR unveils the *TalentFit* agent to de-bias recruiting.
   - Finance launches the *CashFlow Keeper* agent to reconcile invoices overnight.
   - R&D prototypes the *Innovation Radar* agent to scan patents and schedule ideation sprints.

The twelve-month effect of this looks like an exponential jump in use-cases, a dramatic drop in prototyping lead time and a significant drop in IT spend per use case. To make this happen, you can use this blueprint for rapid and responsible scaling:

- **Lay the Runway First:** Centralize data and AgentOps *before* your second pilot leaves the gate.

- **Turn One-Offs into Reusables:** Promote every proven tool to your OpenAPI Skill Marketplace so the next agent starts with a toolbox, not a blank canvas.

- **Form an Experiment Guild:** A weekly cross-functional forum where HR, Finance, and Ops swap prompt patterns, failure modes, and ROI hacks, keeping learning fluid.

- **Track the Flywheel:** Metrics like *time-to-first-value*, *agent-reuse ratio* and *shared-data hit-rate* quantify the network effect and keep investment honest.

Scaling agentic AI isn't "more bots." It's the deliberate replacement of side-projects with a self-reinforcing ecosystem. One that delivers compounding returns every time a new domain plugs into the fabric.

8.3 Practicing Ethical AI: Harmonizing Innovation and Responsibility

As agentic AI spreads from pilot corners to enterprise bedrock, regulation is sprinting to keep pace. The EU AI Act, the US Executive Order on Safe, Secure, and Trustworthy AI, and Canada's forthcoming AIDA all share one clear message: **future-ready by designing for compliance today**. Ethical oversight can't be an afterhours task, it is an operating function.

Standing Up the Responsible AI Office (RAIO)

The Responsible AI Office (RAIO) sits at the heart of ethical oversight; a cross-functional squad staffed by representatives from Legal, Security, Data Science, and Product. Its mission is to embed governance into every release, ensuring compliance and trust by design:

1. **Codify Policy Playbooks:** Translate corporate values and regulatory clauses into checklists a model can be tested against.

2. **Run Red-Team Drills and Bias Audits:** Simulate adversarial prompts, probe for disparate impact, and publish remediation tickets just like security pen-tests.

3. **Own Incident Response and KillSwitch Authority:** If an agent crosses a risk threshold, ethical, financial, or reputational, RAIO can pause or roll back the release in minutes.

CHAPTER 8   BEYOND THE HORIZON

Will (at the launch meeting): "*Paying an external auditor after a breach costs ten times more than funding governance up-front. This office is not overhead, it's risk insurance and brand equity.*"

Nancie: "*Innovation without oversight is a gamble; oversight without innovation is a dead end. The sweet spot is a governance flywheel that accelerates delivery by clearing the runway.*"

Responsible AI isn't a brake, it's the guidance system that keeps the enterprise on course as speed accelerates. With RAIO at the helm, organizations can continue to push agentic boundaries without losing sight of the horizon line of trust.

8.4   Maximizing the Human in the Loop

Well-designed agentic ecosystems don't render people obsolete, they **elevate** the uniquely human touchpoints that machines cannot replicate. As digital interactions spin increasingly through agent-to-agent conduits, it is those **carefully crafted human checkpoints**: moments of empathy, nuanced judgment, and relationship-building, **that preserve trust, identity, and organizational culture**.

Human-Centric Design Principles

1. **The Nucleus Model:** Identify the *critical judgment node*—where human expertise, empathy, or ethical nuance is irreplaceable and anchor your workflow there. Agents then wrap around that nucleus to gather data, propose options, and queue next steps, but never bypass the human checkpoint.

2. **Progressive Delegation:** Elevate responsibility in measured increments; an agent drafts an email, a human reviews and sends. Once consistency is proven, allow auto-send under low-risk guardrails. Yet remain vigilant, preserving human review when identity or emotional context matters most.

3. **Explain-Back:** Every agent action must supply a two-sentence rationale in plain language. If a lawyer, engineer, or customer cannot restate *why* the decision was made, the interaction loops back to human review, ensuring clarity and accountability.

Nancie: *"Humans stay in the cockpit; agents become the co-pilots flicking switches at the right altitudes, never the other way around."*

Will: *"And if the autopilot does something odd, the first officer has to explain why in plain English, not machine code."*

Here's how these principles would manifest in TeleComX's future:

Before agentic AI arrived, a single TeleComX technician wrestled with just a dozen service tickets each week; juggling manual diagnostics, back-and-forth parts sourcing calls, and mountains of paperwork. Today, that same technician effortlessly resolves a hundred tickets without losing the human touch at critical moments.

Imagine this scenario: a field unit's modem flags a fault and the DiagOrch agent immediately gathers real-time telemetry, runs it against historical failure patterns, and even pre-books the exact replacement part at the nearest locker, all before the technician's van pulls away from the depot. When the technician arrives on site, they find not only the necessary hardware in hand but also three clear repair options, each accompanied by a concise, two-sentence rationale:

> "I detected a packet-loss signature matching a hardware failure. I reserved Model X123 at Locker B to guarantee same-day resolution."

This explain-back summary appears on the technician's tablet, so they never lose sight of the "why" behind the AI's decision. As the agent handles the logistical heavy lifting, the technician can focus on the human moments that machines can't replicate. Perhaps there's a student anxiously awaiting an online exam in thirty minutes, or an elderly parent relying on oxygen therapy in the same room. In these high-empathy touchpoints, the technician steps forward, reassuring worried customers, weighing a hot-swap against a quick patch, and signing off on each action with confidence and care.

This is the power of designing with people at the center: agents shoulder the repetitive grind, while humans, positioned at the nucleus of every workflow, bring judgment, empathy, and ethical nuance to every interaction. By deliberately crafting those human checkpoints, TeleComX ensures its agentic ecosystem amplifies human potential rather than eclipsing it.

8.5 Positioning for the Future: Orienting to an AI-First Business Model

If Chapters 1–7 laid the technical runway, the next leap is strategic: redesign the *business model* itself so AI is not a feature add-on but the operating core. Frontier firms are discovering that when intelligence underpins every revenue stream, cost center, and value promise, growth compounds, while risk remains governable.

Five Pillars of an AI-First Model

1. **Outcome-Based Economics:** Price on *impact,* time saved, churn reduced, conversion lifted, not on seats or server hours.

2. **Data as a Strategic Asset:** Treat cleansed, enriched data pipelines as the scarcity moat; invest in Fabric or OneLake so every microservice drinks from the same well.

3. **Modular Micro-Services:** Expose each AI capability, lead scoring, sentiment insight, dynamic pricing, as an API block you can mix and match instead of building monoliths.

4. **Human-in-the-Loop by Design:** Keep lightweight checkpoints at high-risk junctures; they boost trust and create a feedback flywheel for continuous learning.

5. **Continuous Iteration:** Build every service for usage, quality, and bias metrics, then auto-retrain or redeploy when thresholds wobble.

Nancie: "AI-marketing is selling seats; AI-first is selling results."

Will: "And results hinge on data gravity and microservice agility, not a oneshot ML model."

With your organization's business model re-oriented, here's how you can ensure you're capturing value in the AI economy:

Lever	Mechanics	Guardrails
Outcome-based pricing	Tie fees to agreed KPIs (e.g., $ gained per churn point prevented).	SLA clauses define metric sources and audit cadence.
Consumption licensing	PAYGO credits for model calls or embedding writes. Flexes with client usage spikes.	Budget alerts + throttle per tenant.
Data monetization	Sell anonymized benchmarks or predictive scores derived from customer data.	Data segmentation, opt-in consent, differential privacy.

Crafting your pricing, usage, and data levers to pair well with clear governance controls creates an operating model built on innovation, accountability, scalability, and trust; the cornerstones that everyone is looking to balance with AI.

What this would look like in practice is TeleComX tearing up their old "premium broadband for a flat monthly fee" playbook and flipping its value proposition on its head: customers now buy a "Zero-Downtime SLA," with automatic rebates triggered by the Network Guardian if availability dips below 99.95%. They can bolt on modular services like a "Smart Bandwidth Boost" for big-game weekends or a "Churn Predictor" that flags at-risk accounts each metered per inference call.

Behind the scenes, anonymized network-health data fuels an industry dashboard that smaller ISPs subscribe to for CAPEX planning, creating a new data-dividend revenue stream. And to keep trust airtight, any auto-discount over $500 pauses for a human review via Teams, with a two-sentence rationale logged for audit. The result? This could return a stark recurring ARR climb, a massive service-credit liability drop—thanks to predictive maintenance, and a meaningful NPS rise.

Nancie: "Proof that when governance and business models evolve together, AI stops being a cost center and starts printing competitive advantage."

Transitioning to AI-first isn't a binary switch; it's a progressive refactor of how value is *created, delivered, and captured*. Once those loops close, every new capability, be it agent, dataset, or pricing tier, feeds a flywheel that spins faster with each turn.

8.6 Beyond the Agent Era—Glimpsing the Next Horizon

As the ink dries on today's agentic playbooks, research labs and frontier companies are already testing what lies **after** autonomous agents. Three credible trajectories stand out, each rooted in peer-reviewed studies or early-stage deployments.

Swarm-to-Swarm Markets

The next leap from "agent vs. spreadsheet" is "agent vs. agent." High-frequency negotiation networks have begun to appear where microservices exchange prices, capacity, and risk in under 100 ms (blog.sei.io). Supply-chain studies show multiagent negotiation can shave days off procurement cycles (sciencedirect.com), and recent finance prototypes demonstrate semantic bargaining protocols for asset pricing without human brokers (researchgate.net). Commercial think tanks predict a $200 billion "AI agent economy" by 2030, driven by real-time arbitrage across logistics, energy, and compute markets (medium.com). Early academic work cautions that negotiation skills vary wildly between models, making governance and sandbox testing essential (hai.stanford.edu).

TeleComX 2030 snapshot: Four years after the Swarm Mediator agent launch, Guardian agent now messages supplier agents directly. When a heatwave spikes demand, it barters dark-fiber capacity with a rival carrier's bot in 180 ms, locking price, SLA, and dispute-resolution terms without legal review. The contract hits TeleComX's ledger as machine-verifiable code.

Generative Simulation and Digital Twins

Digital twins already mirror turbines and city blocks, but pairing LLM reasoning with physics engines allows *generative* twins: systems that propose and pretest strategies before reality pays the bill (arxiv.org). Surveys of LLM-augmented twins outline a description-prediction-prescription loop where the model not only forecasts but recommends interventions (arxiv.org). Industrial platforms claim simulation speedups of 1000× in aeronautics and electronics when blending deep-learning ROMs with physics solvers (axios.com). Network providers foresee "cousin" twins that quickly spawn plausible variants for stress testing without exhaustive CAD work (walturn.com). Standards bodies expect these generative twins to become board-level tools for scenario planning in energy grids and climate finance (info.ornl.gov).

TeleComX 2032 snapshot: Before committing $600 m to 6G backhaul, executives run 50,000 policy-constrained roll-outs through a generative twin. The model surfaces an unexpected topo-climatic risk in one rural cluster, saving $42 m in avoidable re-work.

Quantum-Accelerated Reasoning

Quantum computing remains early, yet hybrid algorithms are already trimming hours off combinatorial optimization. Entangled Multi-Agent Reinforcement Learning (eQMARL) showed 17.8% faster convergence in cooperative tasks by teleporting gradients over quantum channels (linkedin.com). Surveys highlight QAOA and VQE as near-term workhorses for route planning, portfolio rebalancing, and protein folding (researchgate.net). Quantum annealers are tackling NP-hard logistics problems for pilots in finance and manufacturing, though commercial scale awaits hardware maturity (research.aimultiple.com). Meanwhile, researchers leverage LLMs to design more efficient quantum circuits, coupling classical language reasoning with qubit execution (cis.udel.edu).

TeleComX 2035 snapshot: During Black Friday surge, a cloud-based quantum solver crunches 2^{60} route permutations, feeding optimal dispatch sets to the Swarm Mediator agent in 12 seconds. Tasks that would take the classical Guardian agent hours. Energy cost drops 14%, and no customer waits beyond the promised two-hour window.

Each horizon will demand a fresh governance lens: contractual law for bot-to-bot trades, model provenance for generative twins, cognitive-privacy statutes for BCIs, and export controls for quantum IP. Yet the strategic pattern holds: **unify data, instrument behavior, keep humans at the values nexus.** If you can steer today's agents with clarity and conscience, you are already rehearsing for the worlds to follow.

8.7 Conclusion: Embracing the Horizon

The future of **agentic AI** is full of exciting possibilities, but businesses must remain thoughtful about how they implement and scale AI systems. As organizations move **beyond the horizon**, they must balance **innovation** with **ethics**, **automation** with **human collaboration**, and **efficiency** with **creativity**.

The next wave of AI will not just change how businesses operate, it will **redefine the nature of work itself**. Those who embrace **agentic AI** and build a culture of **AI-driven decision-making** will have the competitive edge in the next generation of intelligent business solutions.

Nancie:

"It almost feels like stepping onto the bridge of the USS Enterprise; futuristic, unbelievable. Yet every sci-fi vision was once just an idea on a page. Agentic AI isn't just fiction anymore; it's where art and life converge. By embracing it today, companies not only supercharge growth but fundamentally reimagine how work happens. The train is already rolling, and missing it isn't an option."

Will:

"Success comes when we stop thinking of AI as a mere automation tool and start treating it as a strategic partner. One that fuels relentless innovation, boosts efficiency, and transforms every corner of the business."

As we bring things to a close, we'd like to truly thank you for committing to investing your time, energy, and open mindedness in exploring this new horizon with us. We appreciate you sticking with us and absorbing the gravity, magic, and science of this agentic AI era and we hope it's either cleared some things up or inspired your next big move. Or, better yet, both!

Here's your final leadership checklist:

☑ **Assess AI Readiness Across the Organization**

Assess and Align AI Readiness

- Audit current AI capabilities and identify gaps.
- Align AI initiatives with core business objectives.

Scale Strategically

- Move from pilots to enterprise-wide adoption.
- Build scalable infrastructure and governance frameworks.

Advance Autonomy Responsibly

- Shift from task automation to intelligent, predictive, and autonomous systems.
- Maintain robust guardrails for safety, transparency, and accountability.

Foster a Learning Culture

- Promote AI literacy and continuous upskilling.
- Create feedback loops for performance improvement.

Design for Human–AI Collaboration

- Keep humans in critical decision points.
- Use AI to augment, not replace human judgment and creativity.

Embed Ethics and Compliance

- Define ethical standards and bias mitigation practices.
- Monitor legal, regulatory, and transparency requirements.

Prepare the Workforce

- Redefine roles for an AI-augmented workplace.
- Communicate opportunities to build trust and reduce fear of displacement.

Measure Impact and ROI

- Track KPIs on productivity, cost, and customer experience.
- Monitor long-term value and adapt based on results.

Stay Future-Ready

- Track emerging tech (e.g., quantum computing, general AI).
- Invest in R&D and keep systems flexible for evolution.

Communicate and Build Trust

- Share AI benefits clearly with employees, customers, and stakeholders.
- Use real-world examples to drive adoption and confidence.

Now close this book, open your dashboard, and invite your first autonomous teammate to the table. The horizon awaits.

Index

A

Adam Smith, AI revolution, 35–37
Adaptive-card waits, 90
ADR, *see* Advanced Data Residency (ADR)
Advanced Data Residency (ADR), 77, 91, 93
Agent–boss, 27
Agent designers, 9
Agentic AI, 3
    automation with natural collaboration, 5
    chain-of-thought models, 23
    contextual signals integration, 21
    future, 147
    governing (*see* Governance agentic AI)
    IVR loops, 28
    paradigm shift, 5
    resilient approach, 26
    solution patterns, 76
    transformation, 15
    transformative, 117
Agentic Capabilities, Leadership Checklist, 71, 72
Agentic characteristics, 41
Agentic framework
    azure AI agent service, 88, 89
    Copilot sudio implementation, 87, 88
Agentic operating model, 76
AgentOps pipeline, 138, 139
AgentRun, 90
Agent swarms
    enterprise-wide swarm intelligence, 67
    multi-agent coordination, 67
    single-agent task execution, 66
Agent-To-Agent (A2A), 39, 89, 142
Agent *vs.* agent, 146
Agent *vs.* spreadsheet, 146
AHT, *see* Average handling time (AHT)
AI, *see* Artificial intelligence (AI)
AI/Agent-Orchestration Leads, 123
AI agents
    adoption checklist, 31, 32
    corporate-level capabilities, 6
    task adherence, 30
    tool and teammate, 12
AI assistant, 14, 22, 133
AI Business School, 125
AI Change Agents, 122
AI Command and Control Office, 137
AI democratization
    citizen developers, 7
    deep-pocketed enterprises, 7
    governance and ethical frameworks, 8
    low-code AI, 8
    low-code tools, 7, 8
    organizational innovation, 7
    risks, 8
    self-service HR chatbot, 7
    software engineering/ALM, 7
AI-driven enterprise, 67
AI-driven pricing model, 26
AI-driven system, 59
AI Experience Managers, 123
AI-first business, 32, 144, 145

AI fluency, 120–122, 126, 130
AI initiatives, 25, 124, 148
AI interaction, 84
AI island syndrome, 24
AI models, 17, 21, 29, 75, 85, 128
AI-powered tools, 5
AI productivity tools, 2
AI-savvy individuals, 6
AI service suite
    Azure AI Agent Service, 79
    Azure (OpenAI + Cognitive) AI services, 79
    Copilot Studio, 80
    Microsoft Agent Framework, 79
AI solutions, 17, 26, 100, 104, 134
AI transition, 3, 4
Alan Turing's Bombe machine, 3
ALM, *see* Application life cycle management (ALM)
Application Insights, 86, 89–91, 97
Application life cycle management (ALM), 7
Artificial intelligence (AI)
    automation and augmentation, 4–7
    democratization, 7, 8
    evolution, 1–4
    interactive layer—serving, 14
    new business models and economic shifts, 8–11
    role-based vignettes, 12–14
Artificial Intelligence and Data Act (Bill C-27), 112
Asynchronous agents, 44
Autonomy maturity path, 135–139
Average handling time (AHT), 30
Azure AI, 60, 73, 75, 76, 84, 100, 104
Azure AI Agent Service, 79
    A2A, 89
    MCP, 88, 89
    memory store selection, 89
Azure Logic Apps, 75, 84
Azure's Advanced Data Residency (ADR), 77

B

Bain survey, 19
Black box problem
    ChatGPT, 23
    demand forecasting, 24
    extra-care selection algorithm, 23
    hidden bias, 22
    interpretability and transparency, 23
    multiagent orchestration, 25
    regulated sectors, 23
    self-service FAQ, 24
    unfair/discriminatory outcomes, 22
Building governance, 106–109
Business Applications layer
    AI-driven insights, 82
    Copilot for Microsoft 365, 82
    dynamics 365, 81
    Power Automate, 81, 82
    workflows, 81
Business professionals, 33

C

CAPEX planning, 145
CashFlow Keeper agent, 140
Change management, agentic transformation, 124, 125
Chat-based AI, 84
Chatbot, 2, 3, 7, 17, 18, 45, 57, 60–62, 64, 80

ChatGPT, 20, 22, 23, 84, 100, 101, 126, 127
Context awareness, 34, 39, 45, 57, 61, 72
Contextual awareness, 17, 21
Continuous-learning pipeline—proof, 111
Conventional system, 65
Copilot, 2, 5, 59, 101, 104, 133, 134
Copilot-powered assistant, 75
Copilot Studio, 62, 75, 78, 80, 83–87, 90, 96
Copilot Studio Implementation Guide, 91
Copilot-style assistants, 3
CRM, *see* Customer Relationship Management (CRM)
Cross-functional teams, 6, 122
CSAT, *see* Customer satisfaction (CSAT)
Cultural readiness spectrum, 119, 120
Culture, AI-driven decision-making, 147
Customer-Credit Risk Spike see triage, 37
Customer Relationship Management (CRM), 8
Customer satisfaction (CSAT), 30
Customer-service agents, 75
Cybersecurity, 5, 30, 128

D

Data analyst, 119
Data layer, 107
Data movement, 78, 97
Data scientist, 2, 8, 10, 18, 65, 80, 107, 122
Dataverse entity, 90
Deep learning revolution, 3
Deloitte, 10, 18
Deloitte Global Intelligent Automation Survey 2022, 18
Designing agents, 32
Designing governance, 105, 106
Digital Division-of-Labor Playbook, 57
 Adam Smith's division, 51
 bolt on guardrails up front, 55
 Carve Out Your Micro Goals, 51, 52
 defining shared memory and baton passes, 53, 54
 map the value chain, 51
 Match Each Goal to an Agent Persona, 53
Digital interactions, 142
Digital noise, 119
Digital twins, 146, 147
Dynamics 365 agents, 81

E

Early expert systems, 2
Ecosystems, 136, 142
Effort-to-impact ratio, 26
Entangled Multi-Agent Reinforcement Learning (eQMARL), 147
Enterprises, 6, 7, 11, 19, 137, 138
Enterprise-wide AI swarm system, 134
EU AI Act, 112, 114, 141
Euro-zone retailer, 112
Executive-level playbook
 advantages, 15
 disadvantages, 16
 pilot, 15
 prepare, 14
 scale, 15

F

FieldCopilot, 69–71, 73
Fleet Orchestration, 140
Forecasting models, 20
Fragile automation, 32
Frontier Firm, 26, 118, 120, 121, 129

INDEX

G

Gartner report, 25
2024 Gartner Survey, 28
Generative AI, 10, 27
Generative simulation, 146, 147
Generative twins, 146, 147
Goal-based architecture, 63
Goal-seeking autonomy, 34, 38, 39
Google's DeepMind, 3
Governance agentic AI
    building governance playbooks, 106–109
    challenges and drawbacks, 109, 110
    ChatGPT, 101
    compliance to competitive edge, 110, 111
    Copilots, 101
    designing governance, 105, 106
    digital employees, 101
    future, 112–115
    hire analogy, 102
    leadership checklist, 113
    Microsoft's AI platforms, 100
    organizations, 100
    principles for responsible agentic AI, 102–104
    roles, 101
    structural, 100
GreeterBot, 56
Guardrail SDK, 138

H

Harvard Business Review, 19
Higher-value tasks, 136
HIPAA, 112, 114
HITL, *see* Human-in-the-loop (HITL)
The HR Help Hub, 49, 50
Human–AI collaborative systems, 7
Human–AI Relationship, 11, 12
Human-centric design principles, 142, 143
Human deskilling, 30
Human-in-the-loop (HITL), 6, 33, 82, 85, 90, 97, 105, 107, 128, 135, 144
Hybrid agents, 43

I

IA, *see* Intelligent automation (IA)
Industrial revolution, 35, 36, 118
Informative agents, 46
Innovation Radar agent, 140
Inside Track blog, 126
Integration of automation, augmentation, and intelligent collaboration, 6
Intelligent automation (IA), 18
Intelligent workflows, 29
Interactive agents, 45
Internal IT tickets chatbot, 18
IVR loops, 28

J, K

Japan's 2025 AI Promotion Act, 112

L

Lead Engineers–AI Agent Orchestration Frameworks, 123
Leadership, 14, 31, 57, 66, 71, 96, 107, 113, 117, 118, 125–127
LedgerLiaison, 56
Logistics Scout agent, 140

M

M365 Copilot, 100
Machine-learning model, 65

Marketing Maven agent, 140
MCP, *see* Model Context Protocol (MCP)
Meta-Quora study, 27
Metrics for evaluating agent effectiveness
  efficiency and speed, 68
  explainability and trust, 69
  robustness and adaptivity, 68
  scalability, 68
  task cohesion, 68
  tool usage and instruction following, 69
Microsoft 365, 78, 81, 82, 123
Microsoft 365 Copilot Blog, 126
Microsoft AI ecosystem, 73, 75
Microsoft AI stack
  autonomous field operations agent
    automated agentic workflow, 91, 92
    layer and toolset, 93
    mid-sized industrial client, 91
    outcomes and impact, 93
  demand
    concept validation, 86
    custom ML Models, 86
    iterate and evolve, 86
    kick off with no-code/low-code, 85
    lightweight pro-code, 86
    managed agent runtime, 86
  interoperability, 82
  layer selection
    AI interaction, 84, 85
    map focused, 84
  REIT client (*see* Real Estate Investment Trust (REIT))
Microsoft's 2025 Work Trend Index, 26
Microsoft's AI Stack
  Agentic AI innovation, 76
  AI service suite (*see* AI service suite)
  business applications layer, 81–83
  data and orchestration, 78
  infrastructure foundation, 77, 78
  Leadership Checklist, 96–98
  onion view, 77
Microsoft's "Journey to the Frontier Firm," 66
MLOps, 40, 139
Model Context Protocol (MCP), 39, 88, 89
Monthly Recurring Revenue (MRR), 60
MRR, *see* Monthly Recurring Revenue (MRR)
Multiagent orchestration, 25, 29, 80
Multiturn interactions, 63

N

Natural-language agent, 39
Natural-language prompt, 9
Network Guardian, 137, 145
Normalize experimentation, 125
Nucamp, 6

O

Omega Healthcare, 10
OneLake AI Fabric, 140
OpenAI, 22, 100
OpenAPI Skill Marketplace, 140
Order-to-cash chain, 55
  Credit Check Agent—"RiskRanger", 56
  Fulfill and Ship Agent—"RouteRunner", 56
  Invoice and Collect Agent—"LedgerLiaison", 56
  Order Intake Agent—"GreeterBot", 56
o-series model, 23
Overnight Ledger Reconciler, 50

P

Playbooks, 58, 106–109, 111, 114, 115, 141, 146
Power Automate, 73, 77, 80–86, 89–93, 96, 105
Power BI dashboards, 90
Power Platform DLP policies, 88
Predictive cost model, 4
Predictive maintenance models, 75
Prescriptive style, 48, 56
Proactive/Prescriptive extensions, 49
Proactive style, 47, 56
Procure-to-pay workflow, 5
Production-grade playground, 89
Promptathons, 121
Prompt engineers, 9, 15, 121, 127
Proof-reading, 66
Prosci's ADKAR model, 124
Psychological safety, 118, 119, 130

Q

Quantum-accelerated reasoning, 147
Quantum computing, 147, 149

R

RAG, *see* Retrieval augmented generation (RAG)
RAIO, *see* Responsible AI Office (RAIO)
Real Estate Investment Trust (REIT)
    Azure AI Agent Service, 94
    Azure SQL-backed data product, 93
    dynamic data retrieval, 95
    layer and toolset, 95
    live updates and transactions, 95
    on-demand document insights, 95
    outcomes and impact, 96
    unified interaction console, 95
"Real-time" insights, 21
Recommendation engine, 20, 21
REIT, *see* Real Estate Investment Trust (REIT)
Resource intensive, 25–27
Responsible AI Office (RAIO), 135, 141
Responsible AI principles, 104–106
Retrieval augmented generation (RAG), 21, 89
RevenueMaster agent, 140
RiskRanger, 56
Robotic Process Automation (RPA), 18
Role-based vignettes
    customer service agent, 13
    executive, 14
    field technician, 13
    sales rep, 13
RouteRunner, 56
RPA, *see* Robotic Process Automation (RPA)
Rules-based bot, 22, 63
Rules-based chatbot, 64

S

Sales forecasting tool, 21
Sales-Forecast Orchestrator, 50, 51
Sales Searcher agent, 140
Scaling agentic AI, 129–131, 139–141
Scaling sustainably, 129–131
Security role, application user, 90
Self-improvement via feedback, 40
Self-optimization, 34
Self-service models, 2
Microsoft Agent Framework, 77–80, 83, 85, 86, 97
Sentiment-analysis, 139
"Set-and-forget" model, 40

Shared intelligence layer, 24, 32
Siloed intelligence, 24
Skill Marketplace, 138, 140
Smart Bandwidth Boost, 145
Smart re-order agent, 21
SME, *see* Subject matter expert (SME)
Software agentic, leadership checklist, 57, 58
Specialization, 34, 36, 37, 42, 57
Specialized agents, 42, 67, 137
State retention, 63, 64, 71, 72
Static intelligence, 21
Static models, 20–22
Strategic partner, 131, 133, 136, 148
Subject matter expert (SME), 36, 51
Swarm intelligence, 66–68, 137, 138
Swarm Mediator agent, 140, 146, 147
Swarm-to-Swarm Markets, 146
Synthetic collaboration, 6
System operator, 4

T

TalentFit agent, 140
Taxonomy
    asynchronous agents, 44
    hybrid agents, 43
    informative agents, 46
    interactive agents, 45
    overview, 41
    prescriptive territory, 48
    proactive agents, 47
    quick reference, 49
    specialized agents, 42
TeleComX, 60, 137–139, 143, 145
TeleComX deployment
    efficiency and speed, 69
    explainability and trust, 71
    robustness and adaptivity, 70
    scalability, 70
    task cohesion, 69
    tool usage and instruction following, 70
Telemetry data, 130
Text-to-speech (TTS), 80
TikTok-driven surge, 21
Toolbox Spectrum, 96
Traction control, 110
Traditional AI systems, 26
    automation, 61
    chatbots and ML-based automation, 61
    fixed rules/predefined scripts, 63
    multiturn interactions, 63
    rules-based bot, 63
Traditional AI tools, 60
Traditional AI *vs.* agentic AI
    automating iteration
        uncertainty and environmental change, 64–66
    real-world examples, 60
    self-directed problem solving
        goal-based architectures, 63
        multiturn logic and state retention, 63, 64
    smarter decision-making, 60
    task robustness
        context awareness = adaptability, 61, 62
        specialized *vs.* singular, 61
Traditional automation
    pitfalls, 19, 20
    strengths, 18
Traditional dialog tree, 38
Traditional operations, 9
Transformer architecture, 2
Transformer-based models, 3
Trouble-Ticket Copilot, 137, 139

INDEX

Trustworthy AI, 110, 141
TTS, *see* Text-to-speech (TTS)

U

UiPath AI, 5
Unified Data Estate, 138

V

Virtasant analysis, 10
Virtual assistant, 5, 27

W, X, Y

Well-designed AI agents, 29
Workforce for agentic AI
    AI fluency and capabilities, 120–122
    change management, 124, 125
    cultures
        fear and resistance, 118–120
    employee experience, 122, 123
    leadership, 125–127
    organizational structures, 127–129
    scaling sustainably, 129–131
2023 Work Trend Index
    Special Report, 2

Z

Zero-Downtime SLA, 145
Zillow Offers, 26

GPSR Compliance

The European Union's (EU) General Product Safety Regulation (GPSR) is a set of rules that requires consumer products to be safe and our obligations to ensure this.

If you have any concerns about our products, you can contact us on

ProductSafety@springernature.com

In case Publisher is established outside the EU, the EU authorized representative is:

Springer Nature Customer Service Center GmbH
Europaplatz 3
69115 Heidelberg, Germany

www.ingramcontent.com/pod-product-compliance
Lightning Source LLC
LaVergne TN
LVHW081450060526
838201LV00050BA/1758